# GOD

# GOD

## by Pandit
## Usharbudh Arya, D.Litt.

Published by

THE HIMALAYAN INTERNATIONAL INSTITUTE
OF YOGA SCIENCE AND PHILOSOPHY
Honesdale, Pennsylvania

7-87

Third Printing 1987

Library of Congress Catalog Card Number: 79-88824
ISBN 0-89389-060-X

# Preface

This collection of essays on the yoga-Vedanta concept of God has been compiled from many lectures given on many different occasions. The reader will need to use his own wisdom to find the bridges that connect one chapter with the next, for where there seemed to be a choice between the spontaneity of inspiration and the logical progression of subject matter, we have favored the former. The last chapter might seem a little "heavy" and complex to the average reader. However, if the preceding chapters have been read carefully, it will begin to make sense. To absorb it fully, one should read it slowly, taking short sections into contemplation many times over.

The publication of the work itself contradicts its fundamental precepts: If you have not personally known God, you *cannot* speak of Him, and if you do know God you cannot *speak* of Him. In spite of this, it is hoped that the thoughts presented will evoke in many a desire to know God, which is the only worthwhile desire that there is.

I am grateful to all the devoted students and members of the Center for Higher Consciousness who have spent many hours transcribing from tapes, editing and typing the book. My thanks go especially to the Rev. Dr. Ward Knights, an esteemed friend, for editing many chapters.

Whatever in this work is fulfilling comes from the *guru's* grace; whatever is faulty is mine.

# Contents

Introduction by Sri Swami Rama
ix

Seeking God
1

Living in God
23

A Glance from the Mother's Eye
53

God Within
87

The Schema of Creation
111

# Introduction

Numerous are the names and various are the paths of one and the same reality. Some call it God, some call it truth, and some call it everlasting happiness. God, for me, is truth, and truth is that which exists in all times--the past, present and future. It is self-existent; it was never born, so it never dies. It is the fountainhead of light and love. Searching for God, without knowing truth, is in vain, for God is the ultimate truth.

A human being, though the highest of all living creatures, is still an unfinished being, longing for perfection, longing for a state of freedom from pains and miseries—and this leads him to seek the realization of truth. That truth is both within and without, so one can directly attain it by realizing the truth within himself. It is possible to do this.

When a human being follows the truth with mind, action and speech, he can attain it in this lifetime. It can also be attained through selfless action, through selfless prayers, through selfless love, and through unalloyed direct knowledge.

Even though there are various concepts of God, according to various religious philosophies, I wonder how a human mind can limit itself to only one and call it God. God is not a particular being. God is the power of powers, the force which is the cause of all manifestation—and when one realizes this truth he gets freedom from the darkness of ignorance.

*God* will inspire seekers of enlightenment to find this ultimate reality.

Swami Rama

# One

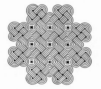

# Seeking God

*If I do not clasp my hand in worship to Thee, my God, then it is better that I do not have that hand. If I see with my eye an object in which I do not see You directly or indirectly, my God, then it is better that I do not have that eye. If I hear with my ear a word which, directly or indirectly, is not Your name, my God, it is better that I am not possessed of that ear. If I utter with my mouth a single word in which is not contained an entire hymn of praise to You, my God, then let that tongue cease to be. In every flicker of my mind, it is You whose flash becomes my thought, and if there is a flash in my mind that I do not know to be Your flicker, then take my mind away from me, my God, but come and dwell directly within me.*

The God of the atheist is one for whom the atheist does not know he is searching, though he is indeed searching. When you take to a bottle of alcohol, you are searching for God. When you are angry and frustrated, you are worshiping God. When you buy a *Superman* comic, you are looking for someone who is greater than you—which is God. When you go into a brooding silence alone to nurse your suffering and self-pity, there is something within you that is calling you to your God. When you go out looking for a dancing crowd in whose collective movement you can merge the movement of your body, you are looking for that collective spirit that is God. When you merge the sound of your flute into the entire orchestra around you, you are merging your individual consciousness into the total consciousness, the superconsciousness that is God. That is the God of the atheist who has not yet acknowledged his search for God.

There is the God of the agnostic who does not know if there is a God or not, but who acknowledges a search because he is searching for truth. And before you search for God, you search for the truth as to whether or not He exists. That too is a search for God.

There is the God of the man of intellect, the God of the theologian, of the philosopher who speaks in carefully selected words, in very clear terms which later on, when he becomes a man of devotion, he realizes were not really quite as clear as they seemed when he was a mere theologian or philosopher.

There is the God of the *bhakta*, the devotee. Someone very near and dear recently said to me, "If I feel sad and have an urge to cry, what should I do with it?" I replied, "Can you think of a saint in the history of mankind or of one great soul in the East or the West who fulfilled his aspiration, without crying vehemently before coming to any realization of God? A civilization or a family in which tears are suppressed is an enemy to God. If you have an urge to cry, let it become *bhakti*, an emotion directed to the sublime. Why cry before a man? Why cry to a pillow? When all your emotion becomes directed to the One being, it becomes *bhakti*—your joy, your suffering, your pain, your pleasure, your longing, your fulfillment. The God of early Christianity is the God of the *bhakta*, the God of devotion directed to the One. *Bhaktas* understand God as their personal Someone.

Now we come to the view held by the Vedanta philosophy. Beyond the God of the atheist and of the agnostic, beyond the God of the man of knowledge and the man of devotion there is a transpersonal God—not an impersonal God, a transpersonal God. We must understand God the transpersonal, the transcendental. We must also understand God whose emanation is the universe—God the immanent. We must understand God as the collective (but more than the collective) consciousness of all the universe.

Every person has a feeling of unreality in relation to God. It is a very strange feeling. There is a part of our being that is always in search for something else; we ask ourselves if there will ever be a time when we are no longer searching, and we give up in hopeless despair, all of us, because we are always searching for something way, way over there.

In yoga the search ceases. The follower of the yoga path states no credo. Instead, he purifies his mind and sees the presence of God within. Of the three stages of prayer—*stuti* (praise), *prarthana* (petition), and *upasana* (the practice of the presence), his is the last stage. Whatever he says about God's nature is from his personal experience of such a presence. "I have seen It. You can, too," he says confidently.

In trying to speak of God we might as well say that to

describe is to destroy. Like all other states of consciousness, the states of superconsciousness cannot be described
because they all are variations of one superconsciousness.
The qualities of gold ore are exactly the qualities of an
arm band or an earring made of gold—the qualities of the
superconscious state are also the qualities, though delimited, of the other states of consciousness.

We have a choice. We can start talking about God as if
He is "here" or as if He is out "there." Many theologians,
philosophers and men of religion today talk about God as
if He is "out there." They advise people to reach God, to
attain God, to pray to God, to go to Him, to approach
Him. But when you *go* to your prayers in a church or in a
temple or anywhere, you are no nearer to God than you
are, say, sitting in the bathtub—literally. There is absolute-
ly no difference between a pulpit and the bathtub as far
as God is concerned. The only difference is in our awareness, in our consciousness of God. But ultimately, where
you are sitting and where I am sitting—anywhere, everywhere—is one and the same reality.

Those who want to consider the question of the nature
of God and where He is found might benefit from reading
an ancient text called the *Mandukya Upanishad*, one of
the ten or eleven principle Upanishads. It is only one and
a half pages long—one of the shortest of the Upanishads,
and one of the most concise statements about God. It is
an explanation of the word Om, a combination of three
sounds: *a, u,* and *m.*\* According to the *Mandukya Upanishad*, the sound *a* describes one level of existence, one
level of consciousness—wakefulness. The sound *u* describes

---

\* Sometimes there is a confusion regarding the correct pronunciation of the
word *Om* or *Aum.* In Sanskrit a + u always produces an "o" sound by a
principle called euphony in linguistics.

another level of existence, another level of consciousness—dream; the sound *m* describes a third level of existence and consciousness—sleep. The text, as well as the tradition, then says that after you have uttered the sound, Om, there is half a syllable that is left unuttered, and that is the fourth state, the superconscious state. It would take more than a lifetime to study this, and many lifetimes to realize it.

Elsewhere in the Upanishads we find passages about God, the most famous of which is: "Neti, neti" (neither this, nor that). Thus, to understand unity, the oneness in which there is no *many*, no *other* but the great *I* is to understand God. We also read in the Upanishads:

> Sarvam khalv-idam brahma
> All this (world of phenomena) is Brahman.
> *Chhandogya Upanishad III. 14. 7*

> Ekam-evadvitiyam
> There is only one Brahman, without a second.
> *Chhandogya Upanishad VI. 2. 1*

> Mrtyoh sa mrtyum apnoti
> Ya iha nameva pashyati
> From death to death he proceeds who sees as though
> There were many (phenomena) here.
> *Katha Upanishad IV. 10*

How is it possible for us to understand this when we are living in a world of interactions among many phenomena? It is impossible for the human mind to remain a human mind and at the same time to understand God. Only God's mind can understand God. Only when the human mind is so relieved of its humanness that it becomes God's mind, even to you, can that mind begin to understand God's mind. So long as you have a claim to your own mind, so long as you say, "I have *my* individuality,

I have *my* mind, I have *my* personality;" then give up any hope of understanding God. And if you do not aim to *know* God, then my advice is: do not merely believe in God. Anyone who believes through knowledge should say to someone who believes through ignorance, "Do not believe in God" because an ignorant belief has been the cause of so much disturbance and war that it is better not to have any belief. This is why the first thing that a practitioner of yoga says to another person is, "Do not believe in God if you have no intention of knowing God personally."

Before we begin to speak about God I have one suggestion to give you. Drop all your preconceptions this minute. When I utter the word *God*, what does it suggest to you? Drop that kind of thinking. Start with a clean mind. Start with a completely clear state for now and forever.

I was born in India into a particular group which had its own interpretation of God, and a few years back, after spending my whole life working for them, I sent them a letter of resignation. The last time I went to India I met some of my old colleagues who asked me, "Do you no longer hold these views? Do you not accept this, our belief, to be true?"

And I replied, "At this time, from where I am now, I believe only in my own ignorance. I cannot make a statement about God. Only when I have the fullest realization, only when I have the fullest possible knowledge of God, will I tell you what my belief is." But there is a problem:

> *Shivam na janami katham vadami*
> *Shivam ca janami katham vadami*
> I do not know God; *how* can I speak of Him?
> I do know God; how can I *speak* of Him?

How many of those who stand on the pulpits have a right to speak of God? And when you do not know God, you have no right to speak of Him. On the other hand, when we do have a personal knowledge of God, there is no way to speak of it, no way to speak of Her. There is no way a word could be found to express that reality, that knowledge, that experience which washes over your mind like a wave, and when you have been thus touched by the great wave, you are a new being. You hardly have the memory of your previous existence. The only thing you can do in relation to God is to devote yourself to knowledge and truth and to the knowledge of truth.

So if it becomes a reality in your life that you would like to know what it means to know God (not that you would like to actually know God, but if you would like to know the truth about God), devote yourself to knowledge of truth. Is there such a state? Is there such a Being upon knowing Whom, upon knowing Which, there is no further desire of any kind? Is there a state in which all desires are fulfilled, when there is no further goal, nothing else to achieve, no other sensations that you would rather have? Is there a state in which there is nothing wanting, nothing missing, in which there is completion and perfection of your consciousness, of all your desires and wishes? Does such a state exist?

We must also be clear about our motives in following this inquiry. Why do you read these words? Why are you reading this book? What prompts you to come to this book about God? What in you is it that is inquiring? What sort of relationship do you have with that inquiry? Is it only that you want to know whether such a reality really exists? The second question is, how much do you want to know about this reality? We shall talk about God later.

Let us now talk about ourselves. How much do you want to know this reality? Do you really want to know it? If so, it is necessary for you to divert all of the channels of your life energies in such a way, in such a direction, that all your actions and sensations become an aid in realizing that truth.

It is not possible to know God with anything less than total immersion. You simply cannot be half in this world and half in the world of God. God is totality. God is absoluteness. Whatever that totality is—if it is whatever that absoluteness is—until you become completely immersed in the inquiry there is no way for you to know God. When every longing of your life is a longing to know that truth, when every experience with your finger tips is interpreted in terms of God, when every morsel of food that you put into your mouth is interpreted as an offering to God, when an embrace with any person is in your mind as if it is given to God, when you turn left and that turning toward the left is towards God and when you turn right and that turning right is also towards God, when climbing up is towards God and climbing down also is towards God, when you are perfectly immersed in that inquiry—then you have some hope of knowing God.

Before that, no. You are only playing with one particular idea, an idea of the limited human mind—limited in time and space and to causation.

Did you think that God's name was G-O-D = God? There is no such name. In the experience of God there are no names, no words. Therefore, if you think that the word G-O-D is God, then by uttering the words *sugar, sugar, sugar* you should be able to feel sweetness in your mouth and not need any more sugar in your tea. All you would have to do is utter an incantation of the word *sugar* over the tea, and the tea would become sweet! If by uttering the words *God, God, God,* you think you will find God, then you need no salt in your soup, for by uttering the word *salt,* you would be able to make the soup salty!

Those who have found God, have done so only through total immersion. Below is a paraphrase of a prayer the yogis sing often:

> You are my own Self, Oh Shiva.
> My intelligence is your feminine consort.
> These breaths are your attendants.
> This body is your temple.
> Every sensation I receive through my senses is
>     An offering of worship to you.
> Opening my eyes is burning the candle before your altar.
> Listening to sounds with my ear is to ring the
>     temple bell.
> My sleep is your eternal meditation.
> Each of my steps is a procession around your altar.
> Every word I speak is a hymn of praise.
> Every act that I perform is worship offered to you.

This statement should not remain separate from life, for only when every breath becomes a repetition of the thought of God, only when you realize that every sensation comes from that one source, only then are you an inquirer after, or a devotee, of God, and only then will you find Him. Anyone who has ever found God has found it through this kind of total immersion.

The greatest statement about God is silence—silence of words, silence of mind. When the mind is totally silenced, that is the name of God. When in the mind there is no awareness of any object, any person, any experience, any relationship, any memory, any impression that is of limited time, limited space, limited sequence—when the mind is totally silent to all of these, then whatever that unnamed, without form, without words, indescribable is—that is the name of God.

When you utter the word *God*, you make a sound that is limited in space and sequence. That is not the name of God. Only when the consciousness has broken all the barriers of limitations, all the boundaries—whatever is found then is God. Take any experience of your life, any sensation you have now. How many sensations do you have now in you? Name them in your mind. Whatever experiences you have now, whatever thoughts are occurring in you now, all of those sensations, thoughts and experiences are in one way or another limited to some thing or some time, to some place, to some sequence.

Can you get out of that limitation? Can you snap out of it? Can you do something that is not similarly limited in time, space or sequence? I would like you to contemplate this possibility. Take whatever experiences you are having—the words you are hearing, the thoughts that are arising in your mind, the awareness of your body, of your senses, of your breath or of your thoughts. In all of those do you find anything that is not limited to a specific time, place or sequence of causation? If not, then break it; stop it; move on to something else. When you move on to something else, examine that also. Do you find it to be free of the limitations of time, space and sequence? If you do not find it limited, you have entered the highest state of consciousness. If you find the next experience, the next thought, also limited as to time, space and causation, then you are still away from God-consciousness.

So where is it? How can you silence your mind so completely that nothing occurs that has a boundary to it, or a beginning or an end in time, space or sequence? How many times in your life have you come close and just touched such an experience of the unbounded reality?

Whenever you come to that, you have come close to God.

Many people pray with belief, but without knowing. Some even pray without believing. When you pray, believing, even then you are trying to reach something "there." In God-consciousness there is no "away," no attainment or achievement. There is no "there," it is all here, wherever you are. So if you think you should go towards a God that is away from you, who is somewhere else, then that idea has to be dropped. The movement toward God is not an outward movement in which you can point your finger up or down, out or in. Many who practice meditation say that God is inside, within. That, too, is an incomplete statement because we live in a world of opposites. We associate the words in our language with antonyms. When we say *within*, somewhere in the back of the mind we hear *not without*. When we say *inside*, somewhere in the back of the mind we hear *not outside.* This is wrong. Neither up nor down, neither inside nor outside, neither there nor here—none of those concepts apply to God. That is why—again—if we want to start studying about God, the very first thing that each one of us has to do is to drop whatever idea we already have about Him. Do you have something that comes to your mind when the word *God* is uttered? Then drop it.

If there is a sponge floating in the sea, where is the sea in relation to that sponge? Where will that sponge go to look for the sea? Inside or outside? Will it go to a bigger sponge and say, "*Guru*, where is the sea?" Will the *guru*-sponge say to the disciple-sponge, "Well, look inside but not outside, above you but not below you, around you, but not within you?" What is the nature of a consciousness of the entire sea? And with what idea of the sea should the sponge begin?

There is a story told in India—we shall Americanize it—about a frog from Lake Superior who went down to the farm country where there were many cows. Where the cows walked they left hoofprints, and when the rain fell the depressions in the ground from their hoofs were filled with water. A little tadpole is born in this hoof-puddle. The frog from the hoof-puddle meets the frog from Lake Superior and asks, "Where do you come from?"

"I live in Lake Superior."

"Where is that?"

"It's very far away."

"Do you have enough water there?"

"Sure, we have enough water."

"Is it as big as this hoof-puddle?"

"As big as this one? What are you talking about, Tad-pole? It's much bigger than that."

"Bigger than that?"

"Yes."

So the tadpole jumps from one hoof print to another hoof print and asks, "As big as that? I can jump across your Lake Superior!"

"No, no, no—not from here to there. It's much, much bigger."

So the tadpole jumps from hoof print to hoof print to hoof print about ten times, and then he says to the frog from Lake Superior, "As big as that?"

"No, that is nothing."

"Then you are a liar. No such place can exist!"

First, we need to clarify our motives in seeking God. Second, we need to drop all our existing ideas about God. Any suggestions I make about God are false ones. Any statement I make is incomplete. Every word spoken about God is meaningless. There is no point in endlessly reading books about God. The only point is clearing the mind: "What do I want? Do I want to know God?" And if you really want to know, then you don't need to read this book. If there is within you this desire to know God, then you must decide on total immersion in this inquiry in such a way that you ask, about every object you look at with your eyes, How does this object look from the eyes of God? With every choice you make in your life you should ask, Is this choice conducive to my search for God? If I make this choice, would it take me directly or indirectly closer to the knowledge of God? If I make this choice in life, what are the impediments that will come in my way of knowing God? If you want to view your life from that perspective, then, when your mind is filled with the decision to do so, inquire about God. Most people have not made this decision. They give one hour of their week to God, but the rest of the time they do not seem to be interested in Him.

I will examine the yoga concept of God from the point of view of the philosophy known as Vedanta, which means, "the end of wisdom," because where all wisdom ends, there God begins. For instance, in the Upanishads there are many statements like this:

One should know that there are two branches of knowledge: knowledge of this shore and knowledge of the other shore. Phonetics, rituals, grammar, etymology, prosody, astronomy, the *Rig Veda*, the *Yajur Veda*, the *Sama Veda*, the *Atharva Veda*—all the sacred texts and scriptures are of this shore; they constitute intellectual knowledge. But the *para vidya*, the supreme knowledge, is that by which that immutable, unchangeable one syllable is known. That one syllable is Om. (*O* represents the sound of all emergences, and *m* represents silence—all returning to the source.)

The greatest exponent of the philosophy of Vedanta was Shankara, also known as Shankaracharya (*acharya* is the title given to anyone of great knowledge, one who offers original teachings); the philosophy goes back to the Vedas, fifteen or twenty centuries B.C. The Upanishads, dated between the thirteenth and the sixth centuries, B.C., are expositions on the truth of the Vedas. Then Shankara (eighth century A.D.) revived and reformulated, in very clear categories, the knowledge about the reality which the earlier teachers had called Brahman. This tradition is known as Vedanta.

Here, the highest word used for God is Om, and a word only slightly below that is *Brahman*. (All statements being incomplete, this statement is also incomplete.) In the Vedanta tradition, too, there are four *Mahavakyas*, or great sentences, or utterances, that are normally given to monks to contemplate on, like a *mantra* (contemplation here is used more or less in the same sense in which Christians today use the word *meditation*—you meditate on an idea). The four sentences are:

> *Tat tvam asi:* That Thou Art.
> *Aham brahma-asmi:* I am Brahman.
> *Prajnanam brahma:* Brahman is pure consciousness.
> *Ayam atma brahma:* This self is Brahman.

The word *Brahman* should not be translated as God, for according to Vedanta this universe of phenomena that appears manifold is, in reality, not differentiated from *Brahman.* In order to know this, however, the ego must be dropped so that the individual self, *jiva-atman*, may realize its identity with the divine Self. The teacher's task is to remind the seeker, "that Brahman thou art" until finally, through contemplation, the seeker finds the great Self,

*Paramatman*, within and says, "I am that; all this is God; I am God."

But which "I" is God? The "I" that says, "my eyes and my ears?" The "I" that says, "I am a male" or "I am a female?" If you say, "I am a male," or "I am a female," you cannot at the same time say, "I am God." If you say, "I am John," you cannot at the same time say, "I am God." If you say, "I am an Indian" or, "I am an American," you cannot at the same time say, "I am God." In order for you to know first and then to say, "I am God," this consciousness of "I am male, I am female, I am human, I am flesh, I am body, I am mind, I am John, I am Jane, I am Indian, I am American," must cease. All of these *upadhis*— false conditionings, false titles that you have placed on God—prevent you from knowing God which is you.

In the process of meditation, as one gathers one's consciousness toward this *atman*, this innermost self, the purpose is to remove oneself from all false conditionings, from all limiting layers. When you sit to meditate, for instance, and draw your mind away from all these conditions, what happens? Ordinarily, the mind takes the shape of the thing it is contemplating. This is the nature of the mind. When you are looking at a wall, what happens to the mind? It takes the form of the wall. Otherwise you could not experience the wall as the wall. When you look at your hand, the experience of the hand comes into your mind. This means that your mind for that moment takes the form, nature, experience of the hand. All mental experience comprises the internalizing of something that is external, and the things experienced become thoughts. So you constantly internalize these experiences, and you think you are experiencing the wall, or the hand. What is really happening is that you, the self, observe the mind which has taken the name, shape and form of the wall. You—the pure self, the witness, the unstained, the untouched *atman*—observe the mind. There is nothing else that you have ever experienced, or can, in your life. You think you are embracing a woman—or a man. False. Impossible! You, the self, are seeing the mind take the shape of that embrace and identifying with it. Whatever is happening outside is happening actually to the mind through the mind. Otherwise there is no embrace, no touch. If you withdraw your mind from the fingers, is there any touch? You are sitting down talking to someone, and the words are falling on your ears, but your mind is somewhere else. What happens?

> *Anyatra-mana abhuvam nadarsham*
> *Anyatra-mana abhuvam nashrausham*
> *Manasaivayam pashyati manasa shrnoti*
> My mind was elsewhere; I did not hear.
> My mind was elsewhere; I did not see what was happening.
> It is with the mind that one sees or hears.

A jeweler was busy working intricate patterns into his silver. A royal procession passed, and the king's men said, "What kind of a man are you, silversmith? Stand up! Have you no respect for the king when he is passing through the streets? Everybody else stands up and bows!"

The silversmith said, "What king?"

"What king?! The king of the realm who just passed. Where were you?"

"I was in my silver. I didn't know that the king's procession was passing." *Anyatra-mana abhuvam napashyam.* My mind was elsewhere. I did not see. My mind was elsewhere. I did not hear. So it is only with the mind that you see. It is only with the mind that you hear. Whatever forms and shapes pass your way, they touch your senses, and the impressions enter the mind. It is the mind that is closest to you, who are *atman*, the self. You, *atman*, then watch the mind taking all of these shapes and forms, including distances, colors, feelings, sensations, memories and all associations. You think that you are seeing it outside the body! Try to understand this principle first. It is very important.

So when you draw your mind away from object-consciousness, what are you doing? You are chipping off the outermost layer of the paint on the wall around *atman*. We say, "Withdraw your mind from all other places and be aware only of the place where you are sitting. Withdraw your mind from all other spaces and be aware only of the space your body is occupying—meaning that now you remove the externalmost layer. Then you slowly ease off the second layer—your body-consciousness. Then you come to the third layer—your breath-consciousness, then the fourth layer—the conscious mind, and the fifth layer—the subconscious mind, and so on until you come to the inward part of the innermost layer. And when the self sees that, it begins to see its own reflection. But even then it is not seeing the Self yet.

So we need to free ourselves of all of these *upadhis*, all of these conditionings we have placed on the one Brahman. *Sarvam khalv-idam brahma*: there are no "many" here, says the text. There is no "I" and "you." There is only *atman*, only the self. How many seas are there in the bodies of a thousand sponges in the sea? Only one, and there is no "other." And when there is no "other," say the Upanishads, then there is no fear, no sorrow. When one sees the self in all beings and all beings in the self, then there is no more sorrow, no more agitation, no more delusion. This Self is Brahman. *Ayam-atma brahma*.

Here we are faced with the problem of ignorance. All this manifold universe is one single expansive unit, one infinite Brahman. There is no other—no curtains, no walls, no shapes, no forms. All of these are waves rising in that one Being. Now if that is true, then why do I not know it? Because I lack the pure knowledge of it. But when I have that pure knowledge, this Self is Brahman.

This does not mean that in your ordinary life you do not follow your normal, worldly nature. There is the story of a disciple who studied the Vedanta texts from his master for twelve years in his monastery, mastered the whole philosophy and logic of it, and became totally immersed in the knowledge of Brahman. Then his master sent him to the city for the first time in his life to face the din and clamor. There, the king's elephant was in its seasonal frenzy, a little bit angry, and the *mahout*, sitting on the elephant's neck, was trying to control it, shouting a warning to everybody in the street, "Watch out! Stay away! Watch out!"

But this *brahmacharin* disciple, having studied all the Vedanta philosophy and knowing all to be Brahman, thought to himself, "I am Brahman. The elephant is Brahman. How can Brahman hurt Brahman?" He alone walked his way in his contemplation, reciting the sentence, "*Sarvam khalvidam Brahma*—All this is Brahman." The elephant gave one huge whack with his trunk and the poor disciple fell, injured, to the side of the street. He got up and shook himself, and his *guru*, who had been secretly watching over him, stood there. So the disciple said, "You taught me that all this is Brahman. How could Brahman hurt Brahman?"

"Sure enough," the *guru* said, "Brahman could not hurt Brahman. But that one who was shouting all this time to stay away and to watch out, why didn't you hear *that* Brahman?"

So the empirical reality of the universe is not denied. As long as you are in the world of the many, your sister is your sister, your brother is your brother, your husband is your husband, your wife is your wife, and the values of the various levels of reality cannot be interchanged as they exist on that level of consciousness. Most people say that one's consciousness exists on the level of the reality of the world. That may be so. But the Vedanta tells us that the realities of the world exist on the level of your consciousness. So where your consciousness is, there also is the appropriate value system. The values of one level cannot be crossed with the values of another.

As the yogi advances from one level of consciousness *(bhumi)* to another, he finds God's many emanations as realities of the mind and consciousness. Whatever he has heard said by the prophets, sages and the scripture he now tests out through mental experimentation and divine experience in consciousness. Before this he may have only believed; now he knows.

# Two

# Living in God

One of the greatest possible blessings that could be given to a family in Vedic times was:

*Nasya abrahma-vit kule bhuyat*
May no one be born in this family who will not know God.

To fulfill such a blessing a family and a society need a system of education and childhood training that is steeped in God, and in this chapter we shall relate the story of the author's own childhood, the story of an education in the Vedic and yoga traditions. God to a yogi brought up in this tradition is a very, very personal affair. To him, the most personal thing in life is God—the only reality, the only thing real; to him the only problem is finding or not finding God in this life. I do not recall having any other problem in this entire life, for all others are seen from that perspective. In other words, if I solve this particular problem in this way, will it lead me to God? If I follow it some other way, will it lead me to God?

A person's belief in God is meaningless. God is not something you believe in or don't believe in, for man's only relationship to God is in knowledge of God. If you believe you have a mother, but you have no relationship with the mother, then you have no mother. If you believe you have a sister or a brother somewhere, but if you have not ever met that brother or sister, then it does not matter whether you do meet him/her or not. That brother, that sister, is not real to you.

You are perhaps expecting a philosophical discourse here, quotations from the texts and scriptures to explain God, but we are speaking of a very personal affair, something very private. It is as private as trying to explain your relationship with your wife or your husband.

One cannot believe in a God unless he knows God, and one's belief in God grows only in his or her knowledge of God. How you perceive, how you experience God—that is what decides your knowledge of, your belief in, your relationship with Him. In every child at birth there is a wordless knowledge of Him. A child who goes down to the flower in the back yard before eating a meal and tries to feed that flower, and then cries and complains to the mother, "The flower won't take the food," knows about God. There is an instinctive knowledge in that child that somewhere the flower is like himself. No child ever tries to feed a table—only a bird or a flower. We thus see that in every child there is a recognition of the unity of life. That all life—in me, in a dog, in a flower—is somewhere one. Only when the word *God* is introduced is God forgotten. And when the knowledge is forgotten the word becomes meaningless because it no longer refers to the child's natural understanding of and attraction to the oneness of all life—the oneness of everything living, everything conscious, everything vital and moving that is God. I recall my first shock in life around the age of four. The dog I was speaking to wouldn't answer me, and I could not understand it when my sister tried to explain that dogs do not speak like us. If all life is God, why won't it speak like me, the child wonders.

Some people are fortunate enough to be born into a very poor home where the only thing that matters is God-realization, where the poverty is voluntary, where the father closes his factories and decides to give his life to bringing forth a son who will seek in life nothing but God. How can one speak of God to those who have not yet sought, searched, aspired to find Him? I recall being taught to pray at the age of four. I recall, even before that, sitting in my mother's lap or at her side, or at the side of my father for the daily worship. The form of worship in various cultures may differ, but worship is worship. In my tradition one might go to church on special, sacred days, but more often we would light a fire, or make an offering of flowers, or burn incense, and the entire family would sit together and follow through the rituals and forms of prayer. The area surrounding the worship became an area of God; that place became God's dwelling. Even though you slept in that room, it was now a place of God. To keep it unclean was an ungodly act—a move away from God—because if you kept the room unclean, then you would keep your body unclean and you would also keep your mind unclean—confused, agitated. If, even at the age of four, you left your blankets lying around, it meant that your mind was totally confused. It could not meditate.

The first thing for me at the age of four, upon getting up in the morning, was to look at a little mirror and concentrate on my own face, on the image of that face, and not look at other things. One was looking at God. In my tradition a child is taught to step on the ground only after he has affirmed his unity with God, so, sitting on the bed, the child recites:

> In this morning hour I remember my own inner self
>     flashing in my heart
> Who is the pure existence, consciousness and joy;
> The fourth, the higher state which passes through the
>     dream, sleep and wakeful states,
> That pure Brahman, that godly divine spark I am;
> I am not this aggregate of physical, material elements.

Then the child is taught to step on the ground saying:

> O, ocean-robed, mountain-breasted mother Earth,
> Sustain me as you sustain all beings,
> And forgive my touching you with my feet.

To step on the ground was to walk on God; to step into the water of a river was to bathe in God. I recall distinctly that to spill milk was an insult to all motherhood in the entire universe; it was an insult to your own mother, to the motherhood in the cow, to the everflowing motherhood of the river; it was an insult to the motherhood of God. You did not spill milk because milk was God. To throw away food was an insult to God because food grows from the earth which is the mother of all—and the primary motherhood is of God. You sat for eating in the same position in which you sat for meditation, and you kept the same mood at mealtime that you kept at meditation time. To wear any clothing was to wear a sacred vestment, for just as the body has been given to the soul, so the clothes have been given to the body to protect it so that the soul may continue its search for God. There was nothing, there was no act that was not an act of relationship with God.

I woke at six every morning and did my first prayers sitting on the bed, a hard board on four legs on which there was one single mat—nothing soft. I woke, sat up, looked at my reflection in a mirror, meditated for five minutes with the prayers that were recited by everyone in the family, got up and did the godly act of washing the body, of bathing the body, to prepare myself for prayer. The act of bathing was preparation for prayer, so the feeling of prayer came into my mind at the same time that I was bathing; the bath created a mood for prayer just as the morning should set a mood for the whole day. If I wanted to sing in the bathroom, I sang; I chanted. Before the bath, though, I went and touched the feet of my father and mother because father and mother too are representations of God. We were taught that a person has three *gurus*: mother, father and teacher: *Matrman pitrman acharyavan purusho veda*. These were Sanskrit passages that we recited and memorized. Mother, father, teacher (ordinary teacher and spiritual guide—for both of them the same word was used) are the *gurus*. We were taught, according to the *Law Book of Manu*, that your own spiritual teacher equals ten paid teachers. A hundred *gurus* equal one father, and a hundred fathers equal one mother. One mother is a hundred fathers, one father is a hundred *gurus*, and one *guru* is ten teachers. All teaching is of God, so your mother is your first *guru*, your father is your second *guru*, and then any other teacher is your *guru*. Whoever is senior to you, greater than you in age, knowledge, wisdom, action, is closer to God than you are; so in serving the mother and father you receive God's blessing because they have more knowledge than yourself; they are closer to God. The idea of reaching God without serving your mother and father was unknown in the ancient traditions. The idea of worshipping God, without giving food to a beggar, was unknown. We were taught that a human being is born with three debts: The first is to the ancestors, the father and the mother through whom your body has come into being, for with the body you can worship, you can pay off your *karma*, you can search for God. The second debt is to the ancient prophets, sages, seers, *gurus* through whom you have received knowledge and wisdom. The third debt is to God in nature, and to God as God. All your acts in life, even as children, are a way of paying this threefold karmic debt.

Every morning we would oil and massage our bodies and do *asanas* together—the entire family. We massaged the feet and bodies of our parents. To me, this was service to God. The word service was so deeply engraved in our minds and in our lives that we could not think of attaining God without serving everybody. Just as at mealtime we sat in the same position and in the same mood in which we sat for meditation, so also did we greet other human beings exactly in the same way that we worshiped God—with clasped hands brought to the heart and the head bowed. We honored God in the human form. Many people are taught to bow to no man. We were taught to bow to every person, for you cannot know in what guise, in what form, God will appear before you. We were taught to keep every place in the house clean because the house is the temple of God—all worship is performed in the house. Every act that we did from morning till night, was an act of worship, of service. For instance, when you are sitting in a cold room and you get up on your own initiative and close a window—not because you are cold, but as an act of humble service to the others in the room—then you are worshiping God.

When I see people sitting and not doing a service that could be done for everybody in the room—leaving food on the plate, for instance, or throwing a blanket down without folding it—I say, "This is not godly; this is not a meditative person; his mind is confused." If I find that the ear of a student smells when he has come for initiation, I say, "This person is not ready to receive God. He does not even know how to clean his ear. How can he clean his mind?" These are habits we develop from childhood. I worshiped God by massaging my father's head, by touching my mother's feet. I received God's blessing by receiving their blessing, and I still believe that any prosperity, happiness, joy that has come into my life must be the result of blessings received from my parents or from my *guru*. Serving my *guru* is to me the same very personal, very physical, service. If I go into his room, my first thought should not be, "What will he teach me? Will he give me meditation?" My first thought should be, "Has he eaten today? Can I serve him food? Is there a shawl of his that needs cleaning?" In the home, the first thought should be, "Has everyone eaten?" That is service and worship to God. If everyone has not eaten, then you have no consideration for God in the human form, for the divine spark within. Will you then have consideration for God in the whole universe? You cannot. So an act of very, very personal service, with as great a humility, as great a modesty as possible, starting right with  our relationship with our parents, was our training to search for God.

For years, after doing the same morning practice, followed by a little breakfast, I sat down for study in the same position in which I would sit for prayer or meditation—because all knowledge is knowledge of God. All intellect is intellect of God. All wisdom is wisdom of God. Every word spoken is God's name. Just as every finger in my hand is my finger, my part, the life in it my life, so all reality, all consciousness, all joy, all pleasure is of God. The existence of a wall, for instance, is in God (in Sanskrit the word for *wall* is the name of a "part" of God). Even the word *spitting* is the name of the godly act of cleansing. God's *potentia, shakti*, living energy, manifests itself in three forms: *iccha, jnana* and *kriya*—will, knowledge and action. Whatever there is of these proceeds from one source, just as every ripple in the sea is of the sea.

The first science taught in a Brahmin family is that of pronunciation, *shiksha*. In fact, the word *pronunciation* is synonymous with education, for it was felt that the mind's greatest force is exhibited to the world in the form of language, and if you couldn't purify language, you couldn't purify the mind. From the age of five on, the very first page of my Sanskrit *shiksha* book, was this passage,

> Oh the glory of words,
> Shining like the stars and the moon,
> Beautiful like flowers;
> Each word a flower, each word a star.

A graduate student writing a paper that is grammatically incorrect was thought to be ungodly, for the source of language is an expression of God's knowledge in the mind. If your mind is not clear, your language is not clear. The second science taught to a Brahmin child was grammar. For three or four years I read nothing but the very highly mathematical *sutras* of Panini—four thousand *sutras,* which contained all the rules of the language, had to be memorized. By the age of seven and a half I could recite the entire text which today's linguistic experts have to feed into a computer in order to understand. I sat in a meditative posture when I recited because in the texts of one debate on grammar it was said,

> Opponent: This *sutra*, this sentence, this aphorism should not be here.
> Proponent: How can you say this? The great sage and yogi, Panini, sat every morning facing the sun in his meditation. In that concentration he brought forth these *sutras*. How can even a single word, even a single syllable, be inaccurate in this, let alone an entire rule?

We were taught that all knowledge was revealed knowledge, and you went to knowledge to receive revelation. So grammar was studied sitting in meditative postures. (The word for the language of our tradition, Sanskrit, means *refined*; it comes from the same root as the word *samskara*, or a mental impression.) The study of language was a divine act. It was also a key to the revealed scriptures, like the Vedas. So for three to four thousand years some Brahmin families have done nothing but transmit, pass on, the Vedas. For four thousand years they have not changed a single intonation because the sound they make when they pronounce a word is the revealed sound vibration, and it must be preserved that way. That, to me, was worship to God. If you cannot find God in those acts, you cannot find God elsewhere.

At the age of six I received my sacred thread, my *yajnopavita*, which gave me the right to study the sacred scriptures and to perform ceremonies, sacraments and acts of worship for others. This means that from that moment on I was a priest. (How much you will do as a priest depends on how much of the knowledge you master.) I remember three days of fasting on milk, and then, on the morning of the ceremonial I wore yellow clothing, for that color represents the root center of consciousness. Then I was taught my first lesson in the Vedic *mantras*, the *mantra* known as *Gayatri* which is taught to every Brahmin child on the day the sacred thread is given. Translated, it goes as follows:

> In earth, sky and heaven I meditate upon and sustain in myself the beautiful brilliance of God who shines in the splendor of the Sun. May He inspire my wisdom.

That is recited at least a hundred and eight times at the time of *sandhya*, the morning and the evening prayer.

I learned to read the clock because I was impatient for the study period to end at twelve o'clock. I learned that when the short hand and the long hand came together my father would say, "twelve o'clock," and I used to wait for that moment when I could put my book down. Then I ate, rested, sat down again and studied. At five I took a wash—feet, face and hands, in that order, because if you wash your face first, and then wash your hands, the heat rises up again. So you washed your feet first. Going to the bathroom was a regulated habit practiced twice a day—once in the morning, and the last thing in the evening before dinner. Then we might go out for a walk with father and mother—or the whole family, which included my two sisters, might go together. After the age of five I had no toys. No one from outside was allowed to bring anything, for any thought, any word might affect our training. Purity of mind was so important.

You might ask, "Was I lonely?" It can be answered as follows: In 1974, when a group of a hundred and fifty members of the Himalayan Institute went to India with H. H. Sri Swami Rama, we visited Anandamayi Ma, the well-known woman master. Someone from our group asked a question about loneliness, and we had to spend fifteen minutes trying to find an Indian word for "lone-liness." I had my sisters to play with, but not toys or outside friends. We played with each other. What did we play? Most of the plays I remember were enactments from the sacred stories like the *Ramayana* and the *Mahabharata* in which I would become Krishna and teach Arjuna, or my sister would become Krishna and teach Arjuna, or we would act out other characters from other stories. I recall the very early fantasies I indulged in after lunch (when we lay down for a siesta). While everybody slept (and I pretended to sleep) my fantasies were, "Here I am sitting before a crowd of people; I am lecturing." Even now some of the words I speak are from those fantasies, from those lectures. Or my fantasies were, "Here is a crowd of people, and I'm leading them in worship." I would do the entire ritual, with everybody singing the *mantra* and chanting after me. From beginning to end, I did in fantasy complete liturgies for worship (some of which I even now perform) day after day after day. Before dinner there was prayer together again. Certain *mantras* were recited, and then someone would lead the prayer. One day it would be me, one day my elder sister, one day my middle sister, one day my father, one day my mother. The prayers at that time were the same as you can hear in any religion.

> God, you are this; God, you are that. You are total existence, you are consciousness and bliss. I see you, God when I see the coolness of the moon. I see your purity in the waters, God. I see your depth in the ocean. I see your height in the mountains. I see your clearness, openness in the sky. God, let that cleanness, openness come into my heart. When I walk through space, knowing you are all-pervading, I know that you are touching my skin. You are in the very words that I am speaking. This power of speech addressed to you, God, is given by you. I do not know, God, where "I" ends and "you" begin. Let it be that in this life, I find you, know you. Om, Peace, Peace, Peace.

The most important thing that was impressed upon our minds was: You are born in this body to purify yourselves, to cleanse your body, your speech and your mind. The only reason you exist as a human being is to know God in this life. There is no other reason for your existence. It is better that your life cease to be than that you die without knowing God in this life. I cannot remember a day when I have forgotten that in this life I must know God, and know God in his full glory, his full knowledge, his full splendor. There is no other reason for existing. You may slip; you may forget; some hours of the day you may succumb to temptation; you may be weak; you may do something wrong. But, some time during the day the memory of God must come to you: "Did I do anything today that will take me away from God? Did I do anything today that will lead me closer to God?" I recall my happiest moments as those when prayers were being said. These were not prayers from a book. We were advised to pray, and we prayed; whatever was in our minds, we prayed accordingly. We read prayers from books at other times.

We are often asked what the difference is between prayer and meditation. Meditation is the silent part of prayer, where words cease and a feeling comes. You recite the *mantras*, and sing the hymns, because they move from your heart, and then you come to a point in the prayer when everything goes quiet in you; all goes silent. With the words, "Om, peace, peace, peace," you feel that quietness and go into meditation. The breathing exercises that were taught helped, of course.

Evening dinner was at six P.M. Then, in the light of a kerosene lantern, we read until nine o'clock. And we always sat in the same posture! If you really love something it cannot hurt you. Sitting in meditation is not merely to reduce emotional tensions, to solve problems ("Because I am upset, I should meditate"). No! If I love my God, I commune with that God. In our minds God was neither male, nor female. God was everything—everywhere. My earliest feelings about God were of the oneness of life—in the dog, in me, in my sister. It was a feeling that some force was passing through me, everywhere—something invisible, something I could not see. Then my father would say, "You cannot see the air that touches your skin." Sometimes in the evening, instead of studying, we used to argue with him on these matters. Before going to bed was prayer time again. You went to bed with a prayer. Everything was done together. Everyone sat together. We did not know anybody else, and we did not need anybody else. You might say, "Are there not disadvantages to this?" Yes, there are some. They are not too large a price to pay for knowing God.

It was around the age of twenty-five or twenty-six that another shock came to me. That was when I realized that not everyone I met was searching for God! I could not understand how that was possible. But even then I thought that there were just a few people it was my *karma* to meet who were not searching for God. It is only recently that I have come to realize that most people are not consciously searching for God. If I am a divine spark, and you are a divine spark, what else is a divine spark looking for? What else can a flame of light look for? Where will it go looking for light? If you are a being of light, where else are you looking for light? In the touch of a man or a woman? In owning bricks placed in the form of a house? In what?

There were moments of ego, no doubt, when at the age of nine I was first asked to preach in the local temple.

The only people I knew were people who were there to hear about God. The only people I knew before I was twenty-three were those who came to listen to one talk about God. The only questions asked of me were on philosophy. I went from town to town in the evenings, lecturing. In the mornings I studied with my father, and in the afternoons I talked to people who would gather to ask questions. The thought of giving a class on God seems very strange to me. In India there would just be a gathering of seekers, people aspiring to know God. A Brahman's livelihood came from what the seekers would bring him as gifts, but to charge a fee for talking about God is very strange in that tradition.

The tradition teaches a person to observe five daily sacrifices. There is the sacrifice to Brahman, the divine, transcendental, formless spirit that is God. The second, *deva-yajna* is the sacrifice to God in the universe, for all deities, all forms of nature are of God. You do something for the fire and something for the water, and when you bathe with that water, it is in living water. The third sacrifice performed is to your elders—you sacrifice to your parents by serving them, by honoring them, by listening to their words, by learning from them, pressing their feet, serving them meals before you eat, yourself. I cannot imagine, if my father or mother were alive, that I would eat my meal without first checking to see whether or not they had eaten. I would first prepare their plates and bring the food to them; then I would stand there and wait on them, attend to whatever they might need. I would do the same for my *guru*, and then I would eat what was left. That is the source of the greatest blessing in life. The greatest blessing that can come to you is if your parents are happy with you. They would give you everything; even if they disagreed with everything in your life, they would give you everything. So remember, if you cannot give to your mother everything she has given to you, you cannot think of God who has given you everything.

Even now, in India, whatever is earned goes to the mother's feet, or to the father's feet. Whatever the husband earns, the first thing he does with his pay check is to place it in the hands of his wife because she is Lakshmi, the goddess of prosperity. If she has not touched the money, it will not grow; the home will not prosper. All the parts of my body belong also to my parents and to my *guru*. All that is of love, is of God. All that is of beauty is of God. The words that you speak are of God. The games that you play are of God. First seek God there on the earth, and then you will find God here in the heart.

The fourth and fifth sacrifices are *atithi-yajna* and *bali-yajna*. According to the philosophy of the fourth sacrifice, a guest who comes unannounced is seen as a representative of God, and the word for a guest, *atithi*, means, "he who comes without making a date." Ideally, one should not partake of food for the day until a portion has been given to such a guest, especially a monk or a celibate student in an ashram. If, in modern times, one cannot find such a guest, some offerings are sent regularly to the ashrams and other places of spiritual service and learning. Similarly, the fifth sacrifice consists of placing a daily offering of food to other creatures such as birds and even ants. Even in the capital city of India, Delhi, one can sometimes see grains of sugar that have been left on ants' nests. One must understand that this planet belongs to all of God's creatures equally and not to human beings alone.

The *Rig Veda* teaches that God can be realized in all

nature—in the mountains, in the hills, in the rivers. "Through me flows that one spirit," it says. If you stand on a mountain and do not know where the mountain ends and your body begins—that is true worship. As you breathe, all nature breathes. As you breathe out, all of the mountain with all of its valleys, breathes out in the breezes. As you breathe in, all of the *prana* of the universal life-force is passing through your body which is also the valleys, the rivers and the mountains. That was the only correct relationship with nature, we were taught. Yoga is this union. It is service; it is discipline. One should not become subject to one's flesh. Its desires should be conquered. Whatever is there in the world is for your use—use but not possession. It is at your disposal so that your body may be protected—and your body needs to be protected so that your spirit may live in it to practice the disciplines, to have more time for prayers, to have more time for meditation—and for no other reason.

There is only one reason for economic or political order—to provide you with shelter so that you can keep your body together in order to use that body to worship. An ancient text, the *Bhagavata Purana*, says of a true devotee,

> His voice trembles when he speaks of God
> His heart melts.
> He cries out in separation from God,
> Laughs when he glimpses a little union.
> One such devotee of mine
> Is enough to purify the whole world.

This is what devotion to God is. Life is a devotion to God. The last prayer in the *yoga ashrams* at night is for a pure mind; it is called the *Shiva-sankalpa* prayer:

That which travels far while one is awake,
That which similarly goes far while one is asleep,
May that far-reaching one light of many lights,
May that, my mind, be filled with beautiful and benevolent
  resolves.

That with which all the wise men perform their actions
And from which the sacrificers perform their priestly duties
  and worship,
That which is the unique, mysterious personality hidden
  within all beings,
May that, my mind, be filled with beautiful and benevolent
  resolves.

That immortal One by which all the past, present, future,
All of this world is held, that by which, through which,
The sacrifice of the seven priests is extended and performed,
May that, my mind, be filled with beautiful and benevolent
  resolves.

That in which the three Vedas: *Rig* (knowledge), *Yajus*
  (action), *Sama* (realization)
The three branches of wisdom are held as spokes in the hub
  (of the wheel),
That in which the mind-stuff of all living beings is woven and
  interwoven,
May that, my mind, be filled with beautiful and benevolent
  resolves.

As a good charioteer controls the horses and leads them on
  the right path,
Frequently holding the reins fast, controlling them though
  they be speedy,
So the mind controls the senses, this which has its seat in the
  heart,
Ever moving, the speediest of the forces,
May that, my mind, be filled with beautiful and benevolent
  resolves.

The refrain that has been translated above as "may that,
my mind, be filled with beautiful and benevolent resolves"
can also be rendered as: "May that, my mind, be filled
with resolves centered on God who rests within me."

We speak of God as a personal experience in life, in

relationships, in areas of learning, study, activity and behavior because God, in the yoga philosophy, is seen in three forms of power: will, knowledge, and action. Those who think of God as apart from, completely separate from, the will operating in us, the knowledge in us and the action in us do not understand God, for all will, all knowledge and all action is will, knowledge and action of God. Therefore every word that I speak is the sound of God. The sight I have is the light of God; this is meant literally, not poetically or figuratively. The light within me responds to the light outside because there is an affinity between the two. The light that I perceive outside is also a little wave of the spiritual light that is in all of us. We respond to sound because within us there is a sacred sound, which is God. We respond to the thought of others because within us there is a knowledge, which is the knowledge of God. All things are a wave of God crashing into another wave of God—God, neither increasing, nor advancing, nor receding.

In your own personal experience, when you move from God in life to God within, you shift a little ground. The ground does not shift in God; it does so in that "me" which thinks of itself as separate from God. So the experience of God initially is the experience of all things you have ever wanted in life—the experience of eating food is an experience of God, that emanation of God which is taste. It is for this reason a holy act to eat. That is why in almost all cultures there are some worship rituals centered around food. When you have sex with someone you are experiencing a projection of God that is sexually manifest, and it is for this reason that in all cultures there are some rituals and regulations for the conduct of sex in life, and when those regulations are dropped the society falls apart. Whenever you take the ordinary experiences of your senses and stop all regulation of them, when you lose the feeling of a certain sanctity connected with them, the personality becomes emotionally confused, not knowing which way to go.

Having understood the sense experiences as a revelation of God, one then moves from the experiences of the senses and asks God for love and peace. Then, as one moves closer to God this closeness is felt as an experience of love and peace. The nonsensual experience of God is, first, an experience of tranquility; the more tranquil you feel, the more of God you know. But the realization of God does not begin without a great deal of struggle. One who says, "I must see God in this life; I want to know the truth of God" is called a devotee, for if God comes to you without any struggle, either it is not God, or you are a blessed saint who has completed all his struggling in previous lives.

It may be asked, How is it that God is everywhere—within me, within my mind—God is the very self of me, and yet I have to struggle so much to find Him? And my answer will be, "It is exactly the same as the struggle of a sponge to try to find the depth of the entire sea." The struggle is only in that level of you which has said of itself, "I am separate from God; now I want God." So long as this separateness is emphasized, so long as your little "I" remains "I" wanting God, there is a struggle, because this "I" does not want to let go. In one form or another, it hangs on, is hooked to something limited and small with which it identifies itself. The struggle is to drop that false "I." If you have not gone through a great deal of despair, you are not yet a fit candidate for finding God. That path is a sharp razor's edge, and it requires a great deal of concentration to walk on it.

You have the other alternative. You can give up your search for God. Will you then be happy? Those who search for God are often very sad at first. They are joyful, but with longing, and in that longing is their joy; in that sadness is their joy. They are sad that they have not found God; they are joyful that they have the opportunity to find God. But those who turn away from that search—are they happy? Show me one who is not confused, who has no conflicts, who is completely in harmony with himself and who has absolute, total, open love for everyone, without selfishness. Such a one is only a man of God.

All joy, all pleasure, all sadness, all longing directed towards that one search for God becomes worship. Why shed tears for something small when the same tears can bring you the whole heap of jewels which is God? Once you have set your goal in life, then every activity is directed towards that search. Someone once asked me, "Where does boredom come from?" The answer is, "When work is not directed as a worship to God, it is boring." You say repetitive action is boring. I say, "No!" A yogi sits down and repeats his *mantra* a thousand times, ten thousand times, a million times, a billion times, and the more he repeats it, the more joyful he gets. Repetition is not boredom, repetition is concentration. When the repetition is done without God, however, it becomes boredom; when it is done with God, it is concentration, tranquility, peace, quietude. The more the yogi repeats the *mantra*, the more he wants to continue it, the more his concentration leads him to the reality that is God. People who are afraid of a struggle, who are afraid of a conflict within themselves, afraid to face their own "guilts," transgressions and failures, should not go looking for God. A brave man who can face himself can look for God. A brave man who knows all his weaknesses and lives with them serenely, and gives of his strength to others, and "washes" his weaknesses by himself is a man who is looking for God. The Upanishads say, when you are strong the most fearsome thing to face in the world is your own self, your own personality. All the fears arise from this personality, all the aggressions, anger and cruelty are lying locked within your own skull. Afraid to open this hornets' nest, you turn away from meditation, from searching for the self, from anything that makes you feel guilty. When you face yourself, then you know the task before you is to "wash" the personality.

This is very hard. There is always a struggle between the soap and the stain, and most people do not want that struggle. For those who are willing to go through with it, the goal is very clear and near, and whatever glimpses you have of your goal, through the clouds, build up your hope. No one can show you a picture of God; that is not the idea. The idea is for you to gear your own self, to find out where your body fits in your search for God, where your eating fits in your search for God, where your sexual desires fit in your search for God, where your job fits in your search for God. Put all the pieces together, and the jigsaw puzzle, then, comes together in the frame that is called God.

If you have never reached the bottommost depths of despair, if you have not realized some point in your life at which you felt completely disintegrated, then you haven't begun your journey towards God yet. But immediately upon that disintegration, when everything you value in life is gone, there should be surrender. The cup of your personality shatters, and at that moment of shattering you surrender your will completely to the unknown, whoever the unknown is, and right there, by that very act, you have found the perfection that is God.

> If you come and lift me up, or if you do not exist—
> If you are not there, I yet remain here
> And shall do my duty and the day's work.
> If I am a husband, I shall feed my family,
> And I will not ask you for anything, God.
> If I am a wife, I shall cook the meals,
> Or go out to work, or take care of the children.
> I shall do all of these things to my utmost perfection,
> With will, love, peace.
> If You are there, then You will know that this is my worship
>     to You.
> This is my surrender.
> Wherever I am, that I shall perfect.
> The rest is in Your hands,
> You who are here—there—anywhere.

That surrender then becomes your "seed" for growing up. Without it, you cannot grow. Are you afraid of the stains you will find in yourself? If so, you will not find God.

Finding God is a long process of self-purification, the constant purging of yourself, and that is where the *guru*, the teacher (in the Catholic church, the saints) come in. If you really want God and there is a search going on within you, but if you have a little weakness about facing yourself, then the expert *gurus* put you through that struggle artificially. They make you go through despair and watch your despair quietly. Day after day, night after night you struggle and say, "What is this? What is this? Why is this happening? What did I do wrong? Why is this happening to me?" You can't stop, and you finally come to the point where you say, "I'm not finding the answer." Then the *guru* comes and says, "I have watched your despair; you have finally reached a  point at which you know you can't find the answer. Now I'll show you the answer."

There have been times when the *guru* has seen a person who, let us say, should go through an experience of being insulted by thirty people in his life. That *karma* has to be paid; you have to wash off those *samskaras*—the *karmic* impressions. Is it better for you to wait for an insult and then suffer from it for six months, and then wait for somebody else to come along and insult you and suffer from that for six months, and so on all the rest of your life, or is it better if the *guru*, when he has got thirty people sitting with him, picks on you in front of all of them? In those few moments all of the thirty insults due in your life are clear, finished. But you don't know that at the time.

The first experience of God is in peace and love, but this is not necessarily the experience of being at peace with others. People think that peace is absence of war. That is not so. The peace of God is not an experience of being at peace with your goals, with your objectives, or with your conflicts, either. It is an indescribable experience of being the very peace, itself. The only way it can be described is as a field of force. What if the magnetic field in a magnet were suddenly to become alive and conscious? In what manner would it know itself? If the light in this room were to come alive and be conscious suddenly, how would it know itself? That is the experience of being in God. In that experience there are no objects; there is no other—not even an "I" in relation to a "non-I"; it is an experience of being all and nothing. Nothing means "not this, not that, not the other; not near, not far, not moving, not unmoving." It is not now as against then; not then as against now; not as if you had lost or found something. It is not as if you have been liberated from bondage. You use the word *liberation* only when you are in bondage, but the liberated soul in his knowledge and experience has no liberation. Only the soul in bondage may speak in these terms, and for the souls in bondage, a teacher, a saint, a prophet may speak of freedom, of liberation from time, space and causation. But when the liberation has come with reference to your own knowledge of this self known as God, there is no reference to previous bondage because there is no previous bondage; eternal freedom has nothing preceding it. This is the most difficult point for a soul in bondage to understand because you say, "Here you are, *swami, guru*, teacher, telling me that I have no bondage, yet you are teaching me to liberate myself from bondage. On one hand you say that I have all the peace and love within me; on the other hand you are teaching me to find that peace and love as if it were somewhere else, as if it has to come through my own effort, as if I have to look for grace." This is the language of people in bondage. But the more you experience the freedom of this spirit in your meditation and outside your meditation—I assure you, this language ceases. It is, then, as if there is not only no future bondage but also no past bondage either, since all past, present and future merge into infinity.

Now all this may seem like so much theory, but when you indeed begin to come close to an experience of God, when you have even the tiniest touch of the fringes of infinity in your consciousness, there is no way to express it. Can you tell anyone about the nature of your sleep? There is nothing to say. It does not fall into any frame of reference that you have during wakefulness. If you have been a living, entire, conscious ocean, even once, how would you tell somebody wetting his toe in the wave in the shallows by a beach, what "I, the ocean, am"? What is not there in the ocean? If you suddenly became

transformed as you were wetting your toe in the shallow-
est wave by the beach, and if you sent your thought down
into the deeper parts of the sea beyond the continental
shelves into the very ocean, and if your mind went out, as
it were, and pervaded the entire ocean with all the streams
and all the tides that have ever been and shall always be,
from the Arctic to the Antarctic, from the Pacific to the
Atlantic and Indian Oceans, if even for one brief second
you were it all, do you know how long that second would
last? It would last an eternity. When you come back to the
world of time and look at a watch, then it has been a
second, but while you are in it, it is not a second but an
infinity. And when you are in that infinity then there is
no watch, no yesterday or tomorrow, no moment of entry
into that infinity nor the moment of exit from it. Then the
numbers are bathing in infinity as infinity.

Do you want to know where God is? When you utter
the word *moment* there is a pause between the *m* and the
*o.* You do not perceive it because your mind is tuned to
gross vibrations, but it is in that pause that God is. When
you utter the word *God*, the *d* does not merge with *o,* it
only seems to because our ears are not tuned to find
pauses. But in that pause between *d* and *o* is the vibration
that is God. When you look at your hand you see first
the curves of the palm and the spaces between the fingers,
but when you look at the finer lines, the space that is
between those fine lines—that is where God is. If you look
at an atom, it is an atom; if you look at one little particle
of energy in that atom, how large is that particle? Is it as
big as the whole universe? But if you take another form of
energy and bombard that particle, what happens? That
particle immediately, through the concentration that
results, reveals to you its expansiveness and becomes the

most constructive or most destructive explosion of energy possible—on an entirely different *loka*, in an entirely different world, in an entirely different dimension.

Many people crave for experiences of the world. Carry on! Have experiences! But what kind of experiences will you have in your lifetime? Can you put your mind into that minute particle of energy which is about to be fissioned in an atomic explosion? Don't look at all the uranium in the world. Can you focus your mind on just one tiny particle of energy? Then, having entered the tiny particle of energy with your mind, experience the explosion of that energy. What happens to your mind? That is the experience of God.

You come to a center, through concentration, which you never encountered before, in which all the explosions of the universe take place. All the universes come into being from one, tiny, single point of God, and that in which all of space that has ever been, all of time that has ever been, all the space or time that shall ever be, that in which all the beings, all humans, all their evolutions, all bits of knowledge from the grunts of a *dinosaurus* to the words in a thesaurus, that in which all the languages and all the words come together in one single point and are absorbed into infinity—that is God in meditation. We express it by a point within a circle.    Draw the circle closer and make it small; you    then have a point without dimension. Expand the point; there is a circle! All the energy released in the nuclear explosion is one minute particle of energy—the point   has expanded into a circle.

To which religion or church does God belong? Let us answer this by a story. There was a saint in sixteenth century India by the name of Kabir. Both Hindus and

Moslems now claim him to be theirs although he criticized the followers of both religions. When he died, the story goes, both the Hindus and the Muslims quarreled over his body, for the Hindus cremate their dead and the Muslims bury theirs. The Hindus said, "He was Hindu; we have to cremate him."

The Muslims said, "No, he was a Muslim; see how many things he said against the Hindus!"

"But see how many things he said against the Muslims."

So they were fighting among themselves: "He has to be buried!"

"No! He has to be cremated."

The story goes that when they finally removed the shroud, no body was found—only some flowers. So the Hindus took half of the flowers and cremated them, and the Muslims took the other half of the flowers and buried them.

God belongs to no religion and to no church; God belongs to every religion, to every church. Every religion began with someone speaking firsthand of his experience of God. Then people said, "Yes, I think I believe that" because the great masters spoke from within that first-hand experience, and all the rational doubts of the listeners vanished. No amount of logic or rational argumentation will lead you to that place.

The first experience of God is peace, the first stage of God-consciousness is a field of peace—not peace with others, not the pacification of conflicts within yourself, between two aspects of the mind, but peace-being. *Om sham*. Om—that is peace.

God, like infinity, does not change. If I have a cup made of clay in my hand, there is a space outside and a space inside the cup; there is space between my hand and the cup—a space within me, a space within the room where I stand. The space in the cup is part of the space in the room. The space in this room is part of the space in the house which is a part of the space of the entire city, and the planet, and the whole universe. If I smash the clay cup with a hammer, what happens to the space that was in the cup? Does anything at all happen? Shankara, the greatest exponent of Vedanta philosophy, spoke of *ghatakasha* and *mathakasha*, the space inside a jar, the space inside a monastery (the jar and the monastery being the body). Space does not change. Nor does God, who is finer, subtler than the infinite space, ever change. That's why you hear the hymns from the Upanishads:

> More minute than the minute,
> More expansive than the most expansive
> Space of the whole universe,
> This Self of the Being is hidden in a cave.
> *Katha Upanishad II.20*

Without having made the effort of unnecessary actions, free of all grief, full of joy, the wise man sees and experiences the one hidden in the cave—which is his own glory, his own greatness.

Will I find God by action, or will I find God through grace? There is no difference between the two because will, knowledge and action—all three—are one in God's *potentia;* the *shakti* that is God, the Mother Herself.

# Three

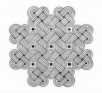

# A Glance from the Mother's Eye

The intensely emotional experience of rising energy which a lover of God feels (a lover of God, that is, who is separated from Him, who does not know that he or she has any love for Him, and who is using all of that energy in whatever pursuits his mind happens to be involved in)—this energy can always be traced to its origin in divine love. A robber planning a masterly robbery, a painter producing a masterpiece painting, a poet bringing forth (not knowing from where) exquisite diction and expression, a man mad after a female body, a woman never satisfied with sex—all of these are expressions of *shakti*, divine energy, the *kundalini*, pouring forth through our *chakras*. But because of our limitations we do not recognize the true source of that energy. It is for this reason that a man of God never judges others and trains his disciples not to judge people, not to be ungodly, for the immense rain of energy that comes to them from God does not always take the direction that we think is godly. Very easily, however, by the touch of a master hand, the great energy of sex, the great intellect, the great inspiration, the great vision, even the great mad rush for worldly power—all of that can be directed toward God *when the soul is ready* because, ultimately, there is only one source of energy, and no other.

There are many who oscillate, like the King Bhatrihari, who is said to have renounced worldly attachments seven times to enter a monastic order, and who returned to his kingdom, his wife and his pleasures six times, who wrote three hundred poems—one hundred poems praising erotic love, one hundred poems praising prudent worldly life, and one hundred poems praising *vairagya*, dispassion. He became one of the greatest names in the tradition of renunciation, but for a long time he could not decide in which direction to concentrate all of his energies. Energy does not mean merely motion, the kinetic form of energy, a lot of movement or acquisition; it means a flow within. Sometimes one does not know what to do with this energy and goes mad with anger and frustration, or he pours it into sex, or produces great poems and works of literature; it all comes out of him, flowing from his genius which is also the genius of God. A Shakespeare or a Leonardo da Vinci receive their power of productivity from the *kundalini*, the ray of God within all. They do not recognize the source of this output, yet it is there.

Emotional energy becomes fits of crying or of laughter; warped energy makes an alcoholic. Armies marching—even that vibrant energy—has a spiritual source. But only when its source is recognized does one become a saint; (the only difference between an ordinary man and a saint is that the saint has recognized the source of his energy.) When you recognize that, then you will turn to the very source of your own power, and the same strength and concentration with which you once planned a robbery, you will now pour into prayer. With the same concentration you once used to pursue the opposite sex, you will now pursue the Divine Mother.

Once again, the first experience of God in meditation is that of immense peace. Gradually, it also becomes an experience of immense energy, well-controlled, for when you have recognized the source of your energy, you are immediately able to channel it, direct it in the right measure without wasting it anywhere. That is the experience of peaceful energy. For instance, if you have a magnet you can have two experiences of it. Most people have only one—they see the pins and needles rushing up to it. But one can also experience the magnet as being like the non-worldly, divine energy which, by its very presence, moves it all without moving itself.

> Tad-ejati tan naijati tad-dure tad-v-antike;
> Tad-antarasya sarvasya tad-u sarvasyasya bahyatah
>
> It moves but moves not; it is far yet near.
> It is within all and yet it is outward to all this
>     (phenomenal universe).
> *Isha Upanishad I. 5*

When the field of energy becomes highly intensified it produces the experience of a great light or of the unstruck sound. At first, in beginning meditation, one experiences little lights, little whirls of energy, something moving—one does not know what. But then it becomes stronger and envelops you. The distinction between the subject and the object vanishes. Who is seeing the light and who is the light? This distinction disappears. Who is listening to the sound and who is the sound? That distinction also disappears. So the involuntary experience that Arjuna and St. Paul describe is one of light from a thunderbolt striking the consciousness like ten thousand suns shining simultaneously in the sky, and you yourself are those ten thousand suns.

The word *soham* comes from a passage from the Vedas that says:

> *Yo' sav-aditye purushah so' sav-aham.*
>
> The person who shines in the sun,
> That one I am.
>                    *Yajur Veda XL. 17*

Thus the distinctions between inner lights and outer lights vanish. Past, present and future merge; there are no distances because that light is everywhere, and you realize, I am that light; I am everywhere. While experiencing your body you think of your toe; do you have to travel down the toe to think of it? No. You look at your toe. Who looks at what? Is the connection between your eyes and your toe outside or is it inside? You are the field which encompasses everything from the crown of the head to the toe, so where others see a toe and an eye, you see "I" alone. Where others see the sun, moon, stars, galaxies, universes, God sees the Self. When I borrow even a little spark of that divine sight, what happens? Can I experience only a part of infinity? This is a very important question in both Christian theology and in yoga philosophy. Can I experience only a *part* of infinity? Many schools of philosophy in India state that one cannot experience all of God at any time because the soul is limited. But the Vedanta philosophy tells us of Brahman, the all-expansive, all-inclusive oneness which is nothing and is all; indeed, so long as you are a separate entity you cannot experience all of God, but when you are nothing but a vibration in that all, then that all is not separate from you. A toe by itself could never know you, but you know all your parts together and you cannot say where the part ends and the whole begins. In God there can be no parts. In infinity there are no little numbers. You cannot know a part of infinity because if infinity were divisible into parts, it would not be infinity. So then there is this experience of the whole, complete, in which there is nothing wanting, nothing missing, and consequently no desire, no question—and therefore no answer, no dialogue. You are instantly elsewhere. Such an experience is the experience of God.

Initially, when such an experience begins, you are overwhelmed; you want to sing of it, to dance, to weave a beautiful net of words to describe and explain it to others. Your listeners dismiss it as nice poetry! (How many people reading St. John of the Cross really experience St. John of the Cross?) After a while all of the overwhelming energy is assimilated, and what comes out of you is not ecstacy, but peace. A mystic has fits of ecstacy. That in the yoga system is the state of *samprajnata samadhi* (a lower *samadhi*), but in *asamprajnata samadhi* that ecstacy vanishes; there are no more ups and downs. The ecstatic joy, the ecstatic expression itself—so very beautiful that it can be had only by someone very far advanced—is still at the level of the mystic. The highest *samadhi* transcends that ecstacy; in that state there is just one unified field within the absolute, perfect, complete master of meditation who is in the *asamprajnata samadhi*. In that objectless, total consciousness emotions do not flow. A master may raise the emotions of others, but he himself has no ups and downs of any kind. You would say, "What a boring existence!" But he thinks of yours as a boring existence because the ups and downs can come only in limited space. But this is not true when you have experienced the *jyotir linga*, the pillar of light.

There is a mythological story in the *Puranas*, saying that once, before the beginning of creation, Brahma, the creator, and Vishnu, the preserver, saw the *jyotir-linga*, the pillar of light, and they said, "Let us find the beginning and end of this." So one of them went downward and the other upward along the column of light, trying to find its beginning and end. They went on and on and on, from eon to eon. They went on so long that many cycles of creation and dissolution would have elapsed, but they found no end to that column of light. So they returned and met at the original spot.

"Did you find the end of that *jyotir-linga?*"

"No, did you?"

"No."

In that infinity where is up and where is down? A pilot flying in the sky does not know where up and down are—he has to rely on instruments. Our conceptions of up and down are so earthbound that even in this very material universe we can reach a point very quickly at which we don't know up and down any more. When that is so in an ordinary sky full of clouds, how much more so is it in *chid-akasha*, in the inner space of consciousness!

The experience of this unified field of infinity is at once of peace. In it there can be no conflicts because it is all—and it is love; in it there are no divisions between you and me. Understand that love. Not the love in which I love you, you love me, but love in which there are no divisions between you and me. It is not peace between two conflicting parties; there are no conflicting parties because the principle of conflict, of duality, of opposition, has ceased. This is at once a unified field of immense light of which worldly lights, no matter how brilliant, are merely tiny sparks; it is a field of energy in which all of the energy of the whole universe is, as it were, in one big toe of God.

People who talk of cosmic consciousness speak from ignorance of God's nature. Cosmic consciousness is no great thing. Cosmos, made of matter, is limited in the eyes of God; it's a little ball; God plays with it; God is sitting, twiddling his toes while the earth and the sun and the moon keep moving—it is nothing! It's very big to us, but we are very big to an ant. Are we God? The ant is very big to an amoeba. Is it God? We are very big for a tiny blood cell, but are we God? Cosmic consciousness is a very misleading phrase; one can accept logos but not cosmos.

> From the purity of the nail of the small toe of Her left foot
> Come radiating brilliant streaks of light
> And all the worlds are seen in those rays that pour forth
> From the pure nail of the small toe of Her left foot.

So say the scriptures.

There is a beautiful poem to Shakti, the divine mother, the divine woman, the woman who is God, the woman who is the *potentia* of the whole being of God. Without that *potentia, shakti,* even Shiva, the cosmic consciousness, is *shava*, a corpse. This *potentia*, the *shakti*, of God is praised in innumerable hymns, and if one is asked what is the difference between Shiva and Shakti, what is the difference between God and His power, the answer is, "none."

> Taking the particles of dust clinging to Her feet, the Creator throws them, hurls them into space, and there come into being all the suns, planets, galaxies out of that dust from her

feet. Only with great effort does Shesha, the snake of
residual being, uphold it on his head during the creation,
and it is by taking those ashes and rubbing them on his own
body that Shiva destroys the whole universe.

The glory of that *potentia*, the *shakti*, is such that one ray
of that glory, one ray of that splendor, one ray of that
light is the *sushumna* in your spine from which you derive
all your power. The entire poetry of mankind, the entire
history of mankind, the works of all the greatest writers,
thinkers, philosophers, are nothing but little vibrations
that have come into the brain from the one ray of the
glory of that *shakti*.

The yogis are often asked, "Why does God create the
universe?" The answer is, "Because God is." I have no
other answer. Why do I speak? Because I know. Why do
you love? Because you have love. Why does God create?
Because God has creativity. What would be God without
creativity? Why does God produce light? Because God *is*
light. Then they are asked, "Do you believe in one God or
many?" A number is not capable of producing infinity,
but infinity has all the numbers in it. You ask why infinity
produces numbers. Because it encompasses all—in whole
and in part. When we see only parts of the whole infinity,
we see numbers. When we see only part of the great
*potentia*, power of God, we see the universe. That is why
in yoga philosophy we do not say God creates the universe; we say God becomes the universe in the same sense
in which the ocean becomes a wave.

If I have the idea of a circle in my mind, and if I join
my index finger to the tip of my thumb, what do I have?
A circle. Did I create the circle or did I become the circle?
There is no difference between the two. I become the
circle, so I create it; I create the circle, so I become a

circle in a part of me. The first creation is in consciousness; it is in the mind: I have the idea of a circle. That idea must manifest itself; otherwise the idea is of no use. So long as the circle that I produce by joining my thumb and forefinger knows itself to be separate from the idea, then it is separate—apart from the archetype of circle in my head which is all circles in the whole universe. So long as this circle of my thumb and forefinger remains separate from the circle in my mind, it is small, tiny, and it asks, "Why was I created?" But when it knows its relationship to that circle which is in my mind the question no longer arises, because when I think of the pure circle and not a specific circle, then it is all the circles of the whole universe that I am thinking of, and from that whole circle arises one, single, small circle. Then is this circle destroyed when I separate my finger from my thumb? If I draw a circle on a blackboard and then wipe it off, how many circles are destroyed? Is the circularity in the universe destroyed by it? Is the idea of a circle destroyed?

The circles are all there; they will continue to manifest from the unmanifest. The entire universe, with all of its waves and vibrations, with all of its men, women, limitations, interactions between those limitations (the same interactions are painful to some, pleasant to others, but ultimately they are neither painful nor pleasant)—all of those exist in that one *omnipotentia*, all-power, the *shakti* of the Divine. That from which all of this appears, in which all of this exists, into which all of this is dissolved, that one is known as Brahman, the unconditional, the unconditioned, the unqualified, unlimited, *nirguna*—without attributes, without name, without form, without title, size or shape. That is Brahman.

The yogi in his meditation knows that Brahman, and

by knowing that Brahman, the whole, he knows all the parts if he wants to know them. The Vedanta philosophers have always used the analogy of space to explain Brahman. *"Om, kham Brahman,* Om is space, Brahman." If I take a jar in my hand and move toward you, what happens to the space that is inside the jar? Does it move? Does it come to you as the jar moves from here to there? I have space in my nostrils, stomach and mouth; if I move from here to there to you, what happens to the space inside me? Does the space come along with me, or is it left behind? If all the people in a city take their cars (cars are enclosed spaces) and drive off, do they take that much space away? After they have gone off, is there that much less space left in the city? You can see how easily all your laws of three dimensions are destroyed, how easily they become inapplicable. No country, no customs office checks your suitcase to see if you are taking empty space. The laws of the grosser levels are not applicable to the finer levels. For this reason Brahman is compared with *akasha,* space. You do not measure the space in a suitcase, or in the car, and put a price tag on it, but when you purchase a lot of land, not only does the land become your private property, so also does all the space above it! You can't take that space away, but it still becomes your private property! If somebody came onto that space, somehow elevated one or two feet above the ground, would you allow him to be there if he says, "I am not occupying the land you have bought, I am only in the space above it which cannot be measured." It is a paradox—measurable yet not measurable.

That which makes the unmeasurable measurable is called *maya*—it is like a magic show. The space is not measurable, yet it is measured *in your mind.* Whenever you draw away from the infinite consciousness to the idea of any finite part, you immediately enter from the consciousness of Brahman into the world of *maya*, and that *maya* is the mother of the universe—*Mahamaya*, the great *maya*. That is also the *shakti*, the creative power. In fact, some of our texts have said that the creative power is the negative power of God; it is the negative charge of the universe because when you measure, you negate all else— you reduce the infinite to numbers. That power of reducing the consciousness to something less than the infinite is *maya*.

When Brahman in its infinite consciousness knows all of its potential, all of its *shakti* at once without past, present, future, it is Brahman. But when that very Brahman knows that in all power there are many powers, the moment the word *many* occurs, it becomes *maya*. When all is reduced to many, and when from that many you take one, then you have relationships between that *one* and any other *one*—you have relationships between different parts of the manifold. Then, when those parts and the manifold all fold back like a dream folding back into its creator, dissolving, then it is Brahman again. The reason the universe is said to be a dream of God is because it is the result of the same process that you go through when you create a dream. What happens to the dream figures? They are lying in the unmanifest field of your consciousness, then they appear as your own *maya*, and then they submerge again. You open your eyes, and there are no more dream palaces and no streets, no fighters and no spectators. In the undiversified, unqualified *nirguna*, free of *gunas*, free of attributes, indescribable, unwounded, unchanged, not of the past, present and future, yet mastering all time—in that consciousness of the highest meditation the manifold no longer appears; the divisions of

space are no longer there—all space, all Brahman is experienced at once, and that experience is within the reach
of everyone. If you take hold of a single thread of your
energy, the thread of any thought, the thread of any
experience and go to its source, you reach Brahman.

Now there comes the question of whether or not there
is one God or many gods. One Brahman, through *maya*,
produces *prakriti*, the very nature of this universe which is
threefold: *sattvic, rajasic* and *tamasic*. The Bhagavad Gita
says, "My *maya* is my *prakrti*; that is my nature; nature is
my *maya*, my magic." So the little fields produced from
the one great all-encompassing field can be as many as
you want to make. There is a *shakti* to inspire wisdom;
it is a *shakti* of that one Brahman. There is a *shakti* to
inspire desire and passion; there is a *shakti* to dissolve;
there is a *shakti* to help prosper. All of these *shaktis*—
areas of consciousness, linked to Brahman but operating in
their own specific fields—are called "gods," "deities,"
male or female. When Brahman, which is transcendental,
beyond, becomes the God of the whole universe, and having created the universe pervades it, the universe becomes
its body the way you, the spirit, have a physical body.
Then that God is called *Ishvara*, the ruler, the lord, the
master, of whom this entire universe is the body. When
you do not make reference to the universe-body (which is
but one twiddling toe of Brahman), the Brahman is understood as unqualified, without limitations or forms, but
when that Brahman sends forth a spark to permeate the
universe that it has created, the universe becomes its body
and the spark that then pervades the universe is known as
*Ishvara*, the personal god. Then that *Ishvara*, the personal
god, may incarnate, may become flesh from time to time,
from place to place, from planet to planet, world to world.

He becomes flesh to fulfill many missions among many races, many nations, speaking many languages; then that one is known as an *avatara*, the descendent of the divine (God becoming flesh). The *siddhas*, the masters, are those *jivas* (individual souls) who have risen and reached the realization of their unity with the divine. Whether you have the descent of God or the ascent of man, at a certain point, you cannot distinguish between who ascended and who descended because they are both in the same place. So the question of how much in Christ is God and how much man, or whether Christ and Krishna were just great men who ascended to godhood or God Himself descending, becoming flesh, is meaningless because ultimately, in the highest realization of being, there is no ascent nor descent.

The most poetic and lyrical work of metaphysical teaching in Sanskrit is entitled, *Yoga-vasishtha*—yoga as taught by the sage Vasishtha to Rama, the divine incarnation. It comprises approximately 27,000 verses, and here we will paraphrase some chapters from it:

> Once upon a time when I was the pure sky of consciousness, in that sky of consciousness arose the moonlight of awareness. I was then Brahman. I, the Brahman, meditated upon my own being, my own nature, with the cool moonlight of awareness in the sky of consciousness that I was. During one of these meditations upon my own pure, skylike, formless being, I noticed a tiny sprout of will called the will to creation. Just as a seed, planted in a flowerpot placed outside in the courtyard, begins to sprout when the rains fall, so the rain of my attention, my concentration, fell upon the seed of the will to create, and that seed began to sprout. Just as when,

in deep sleep, the attention suddenly falls upon the seeds of creativity, and there sprouts a dream (and when the attention is withdrawn, the dream is folded back again and the person returns from sleep into wakefulness), so I see this universe unfolding as a dream within me who am the sky of consciousness.

As this rain of attention, volition, fell on the will to create, I saw within myself Earth, so with my attention I permeated this Earth, and I became the islands, the mountains, the grass, the trees. I became the minerals, the jewels, the gold and shining silver. Oh so many forests and trees, branches and twigs became my hairs; my body was filled with jewels; my body was ornamented with cities and villages and other habitations. I, having assumed the form of Earth, was filled with rivers, forests, seas, directions —east, west, north, south. I became the one on whom so many creatures roamed. The lilies bloomed on my body; the vines and creepers grew on me; the rivers and lakes were in the hair-roots of me—all of this network, consisting of duality, is in fact tranquil, nondual.

On this earth I paid attention to the waters, and thereby through that attention in the sky of consciousness I also became waters—clear like sapphire. Then I, in my body of waters, rose and became clouds and gamboled in love-play with my wife, the lightning, becoming the taste of all things in the universe. I became so diversified that in trillions of creatures I became the essence of millions of their taste buds. Such pleasure of being water was mine, but I do not believe even that to be the experience of taste buds, but just this pure Self assuming that particular form. With my water body I have taken rides on the chariot of winds, and in the clear lanes of the sky I have roamed like fragrance. Though I am the pure conscious being, in order to see what the experience of being water is, within my own consciousness, I reduced the degree of my totality of consciousness and experienced the consciousness only of being water.

I became fires—an illumination, a light, a brilliance: I became the brilliance of the moon; I became the splendor that is in the sun; I became the light that is in the stars; I became the warmth that is in the fires. Because illumination consists predominantly of the quality of *sattva*, the visibility of all things, therefore, was my limbs. I became the father, giving birth to the white, blue and rosy colors—all of them that sleep in the lap of their father, the light. With my illumination I became the mirror for my brides, the parts of the sky, the directions. I became the power of the winds to remove the mists of the night. I was the life essence of the moon, the sun and the fires. I became the color in gold, in the emerald, in the ruby. With that power of illumination I became valor in man, and in the rainy season I became the lightning. With my power of brilliance I became the god Indra's weapon to split apart the heads of the demons of darkness, and I became the courage in the heart of the lion. I became the fearlessness in the limbs of the warrior in the battlefield, the courage that can break through the strongest armor. Besides all this, I was also in my form as the sun, and I spread out my hands as rays and grabbed the mountaintops on the earths of all the universes.

Within that illumination-form of mine this whole
Earth, to me, looked like a tiny village seen from a
very high mountaintop.

When I took the form of the moon (as I was the
illumination of the moon), I became a lake filled
with *amrita*, the drink of immortality. I was the
face of the beautiful lady called the Heavenly
World. When I scattered myself on Earth in the form
of the moonlight I was like the laughter of the lady
called Night. And I was a little candle, too, for all
the human beings walking around at night. In the
form of fire I became a conflagration and burned
forest upon forest. I created sounds that frightened
many creatures who scampered in the shade of
those trees. But then I was also the ritual fire who
gathered sacrifices made by the people, and as such
I turned those sacrifices into finer essences and
passed them on to the gods of the subtler worlds.
Sometimes I was in a blacksmith's shop changing the
forms of iron into hammers;  sometimes I was a
mere spark. All of this I have been, my disciple.

With my attention passed on to that will of
creativity, I became the winds. I made all the vines,
creepers and leaves dance. I gathered the fragrances
of lilies, roses and other flowers and scattered them
to the wide world; I came into the parks full of
freshness and carried their freshness to the cities; I
slept on the bed of clouds; I dried the sweat of the
tired human beings; I was the fragrance of the
flower called the Sky. I was, as it were, a twin
brother to the sounds that arise in space. I became
the source of vitality moving and flowing in the
limbs of all living beings, carrying fluids in their

arteries; I was the thief plundering the jewels called the fragrances hidden deep inside the flowers. I had the power to pick up the mountains from their roots and scatter them. Such a powerful wind, too, I became! I turned water into ice, dried the mud, carried the clouds, moved the blades of grass, wafted fragrances from here to there and reduced the heat in the bodies of those who suffered.

In this form of earth, water, fire, air I have lived in the bodies of trees, and in the form of trees I have sent down roots to suck the subtlest juices of food and moisture lying deep in the earth, and I have tasted them. I have tasted the way the tree tastes that moisture deep in the earth. I have lain about on the arctic snow. I have sung along with the cranes in the lotus forests. Through my will the suns and stars, taking all kinds of colors, have dwelt in my body. In my awareness of being the entire space of consciousness, I have gathered and worn the seven worlds as that many bangles around my wrists. When I was this whole universe, the very deepest parts of the earth were as the soles of my feet, and the top of this earth was, as it were, my belly, and the blue sky of Earth was my forehead. And yet, in all of these manifold forms, as I dwelt as the earth, as the water, as the fire, as the space, as the illumination, as the entire universe, I have never for one moment abandoned my true nature, my being pure consciousness.

I have taken all of these forms just as the pure power of consciousness alone creates all the cities in the dream. Yet the power of consciousness is not lost, and that dream and those dream cities are merely a mode, merely a note in the music of consciousness that has not thereby abandoned its nature of being music. So all of this *maya* I have created, I have become. But I have not changed thereby.

*Yoga-vasishtha, Nirvana section II. 89-93*

When we conceive of time we normally think of *was, is, will be,* but how far that "was," "is," and "will be" extends is a very confusing matter, because if you look carefully you will not find any clear definition of past, present and future. For example, let us take the present tense. When you have uttered *pre-* it is already past and *-sent* is yet to come. Where is the present? And when you have reached *pres-* the *pres* is past and the *-ent* is future. So where is the present? We are living in a universe which exists on many, many levels of reality—times within times beyond times within times; spaces within spaces beyond spaces within spaces. Because of the habits of our minds and the obscuring veils placed on our consciousness, we have taken the vast, infinite spaces of consciousness and rolled and folded them over. We have created universes; we have created suns, moons, stars, our worlds, our countries, nations, histories, peoples, individuals, families, relationships, problems, confusions, knowledge and ignorance, vice and virtue, conquest and defeat, but looking at it all from the vantage point of the infinite consciousness, we can see it all differently. Let us hold one end of a nearby empty space, and fold it! This is the entire reality of our universe—all that we see, we see in a space called *cidakasha*, the space of consciousness. All the warps and folds of the outer space are first warps and folds in our consciousness.

This idea (that the spaces which are folded and warped

in our consciousness are the universe) has the technical name, *maya*. *Maya*, again, is the ability of the consciousness to measure that which cannot be measured, to fold that which cannot be folded, to unfold that which cannot be unfolded, to warp that which cannot be warped, to unwarp that which was never warped, and from this vantage point come all the ancient stories from beyond space and time. For instance, only recently, about a hundred or so years ago, scientists in the West began to think that perhaps this Earth was more than five thousand years old. Up to that time, from the time of Adam to Christ was thought to be three thousand years, then from Christ to us was two thousand years, so that makes five thousand—that was supposed to be the extent of the history of the planet, Earth! Today we think of the age of the whole universe, including Earth, in terms of billions of years. But the ancient philosophers of India, who did not have our astronomical instruments at their disposal and who explored outer space only within the spaces of inner consciousness, nevertheless came to certain conclusions about space and time that are mind-boggling for today's physicist, so accurate were they.

People ask sometimes how long would it take to be liberated if they meditated every day? And the answer is: one glance from Mother Shakti, one glance from the mother of the universe—just one glance from her, and you'd be liberated! How long is one glance from the mother of the universe? The question is answered in *Spanda*, a special branch of the yoga philosophy, developed in Kashmir between the eighth and twelfth or thirteenth centuries A.D. The basic concept in this sytem is a *spanda*, the universal vibration, and according to it the whole universe is a vibration. In other words, you are a composition of many vibrations at many levels—vibrations of pure consciousness, vibrations of warped consciousness, vibrations of the great superconscious mind, vibrations of the limited individual mind. In the limited individual mind are vibrations of your unconscious mind, the vibrations of your conscious mind, the vibrations of your sense consciousness, the vibrations of your brain, the vibrations of your nerve impulses, and the vibrations of the molecules that compose the cells of your body. The whole universe was regarded by the seers from the Vedic times in terms of veils upon veils of light, layers upon layers of light, spaces warped on spaces, spaces folded back on spaces—and this was long before Einstein thought of curved spaces. In such consciousness, how long is a long time? The philosophers of *Spanda* spoke of four levels of time. Translated roughly they are:

| | |
|---|---|
| Microcosmic | I-time. |
| Macrocosmic | I-time. |
| Microcosmic | It-time. |
| Macrocosmic | It-time. |

Microcosmic I-time is that minutest movement of time that my consciousness is capable of grasping. This is measured in terms of a *matra*—which means both a measure of and the time it takes to utter a vowel (not a consonant because a consonant cannot be uttered without a vowel). The consonants are regarded in this philosophy as males, or dependent beings, and the vowels are the *shakti* of speech and are feminine, independent sources of energy. The finest possible experience of subjective time is measured in terms of the vibrations made when you utter the sound of a vowel—not vocally, but mentally. The time it takes to *think* the sound of a short vowel is its *matra*, the psychic measure or value, a single syllabic time unit. A yogi's concentration is so refined that he may perceive even a six-hundredth part of that syllabic mental vibration, and the time that elapses in such a perception is termed microcosmic I-time.

Now let us examine macrocosmic time. The great infinite consciousness comes into the whirls of *maya* and begins to measure that which cannot be measured. So he contemplates, saying, Let me create space, and when he creates space, the idea of measuring becomes a delimitation. The whole universe is nothing but an idea called measuring within the immeasurable. Thus he creates, within his consciousness, a world, and this moving and unmoving world is surrounded and filled with layers upon layers of the five elements. We paraphrase again from the *Yoga-vasishtha.*

> This is the circumference of the earth. Ten times as much as the earth is the waters; ten times as much as the waters is the light; ten times as much as the light is the air; ten times as much as the air is the sky belonging to this planet. This is one fruit, one single fruit, this Earth. There is a branch on which hang a thousand such fruits. There is a tree which has thousands of such branches, each of them carrying a thousand fruits. There is a forest which has thousands upon thousands of such trees, each of which has thousands of such branches, each of which branch carries a thousand such fruits. Here is this, the circumference of the earth, which is the core of the fruit; there is ten times as much water around it, ten times as much illumination around that, ten times as much air around that and ten times as much

space around that. There is one huge, gigantic mountain where there are thousands of such forests. There is a continent where there are thousands of such mountains, and on that continent there are lakes and rivers without count. There is one such earth—not yours. There is one such universe where there are thousands of such earths. If you want to expand your consciousness then do so, and see how far you can reach. See how much space the awareness inside your skull can enfold. That is one universe. There are uncountable such universes in a *brahmanda*, an egg of God. And that is only one egg. There is no end to such *brahmandas*. And that sea, that megaocean on which uncountable such *brahmandas* are floating has no limit—yet it is calm and tranquil.

That ocean we have just spoken of is merely a wave; it goes on and on . . . . That ocean is merely a wave on a great ocean of consciousness, and that great ocean is in the belly of the cosmic person known as the *purusha*.

Beyond this cosmic man is the *paramapurusha*, the supreme person who carries around his neck a necklace of beads. In each bead is one such cosmic man. Millions of such great persons are flashing like waves of awareness in a vast solar orb, and that vast solar orb is Brahman, the totality of absolute existence, consciousness and bliss. How far does that space extend? How far does that time extend? How far can your consciousness go to settle on which one of those persons, which one of those megaoceans, which one of those little oceans in which there are a million such universes?

Look at it another way, disciple. All of this description of the vastness of universe upon universe that I have given to you—look there at a little beam of light coming through a hole in the wall, and you will see tiny motes in this beam of light. In the light of the sun there is the Brahman; in a beam of that light there is one mote. In that mote are millions of these supreme beings wearing for beads so many cosmic men. In the belly of each is the great, grand cosmic megaocean, a wave of which is that ocean on which float all these *brahmandas*, or eggs of God. All of this is in one mote in the beam of light of the great consciousness called Brahman.

My disciple, when you know yourself to be pure consciousness, then you will be that sun in one beam of whose light there are millions of motes—and in each mote there are these millions upon millions of smaller to larger unfolding universes.

Once upon a time, as this beam of light fell on one corner of one of these motes, on one of these universes within the motes, on one tiny molehill called Earth, in one little hole in that molehill I used to dwell. I have taken many such births from molehill to molehill. My dear disciple, you do not recall all your births as I recall mine. I was once blessed with a long life. Once upon a time I was so blessed with a long life that when the whole universe was dissolved there remained only the cosmic ocean, and in it remained I floating alone—on that ocean into which the entire universe was dissolved. For I was blessed with such a long life that even if the universes were dissolved I would continue to be. As I floated on that cosmic ocean countless ages must have passed, for there was no way for me to count the ages (for the ages are counted when there are suns and moon and stars, but here there was only the primordial waters from which all else is born). I floated on these primordial waters, ages upon ages upon ages upon ages, cursing myself for having been blessed with such a long life that I would not even die when the universes were dissolved. One day or night (for now the days and nights were simply in my imagination) I saw from a great distance a tree known as *ashvattha.*

The Sanskrit word *ashvattha* means *na shvas sthata—* that which shall not last till tomorrow. That is the holy tree of India. It is an upside down tree whose branches are below and whose roots are above! From its branches it sends down strands like a beard that becomes rooted into the ground and continues to grow thicker. It is the longest-lasting tree. Some of these trees are thousands of years old, and the yogis called them "that which shall not last until tomorrow" because even such a long-lasting tree has a tomorrow when it will not be, when it shall cease to be, and on its own tomorrow, it will die. There is a greater cosmic analogy to that tree found in the Bhagavad Gita: "There is a tree, the cosmic tree, whose roots are up, the branches below." The roots are in God, and we are the branches. The *Yoga-vasishtha* continues:

So I was floating in that cosmic ocean ages upon countless, unimaginable ages. I saw an *ashvattha*, the upside down tree with roots up and branches below, and I swam towards it. Wonder of wonders, when I thought I was the only living creature, I saw a little baby; a tiny infant I saw on a huge leaf of this tree.

The Sanskrit word for infant is *shishu* which means, "He who sleeps exceedingly, continuously." Dissolution is the sleep of God, so God sleeps and becomes, as it were, an infant.

Elsewhere we read:

> *Kararavindena padaravindam*
> *Mukharavinde viniveshayantam,*
> *Vatasya patrasya pute shayanam*
> *Balam mukundam shirasa namami.*

> Pulling his toe with his hand
> And placing it in his mouth
> Sleeping on a leaf of *ashvattha*,
> To that infant lord I pay homage
> With my head bowed.

As I reached the baby, he took his toe from his mouth and yawned, and the yawn was so great that it sucked me into the baby's belly. The period of dissolution seemed to be over after I was sucked in because here, in the belly of the sleeping infant, I saw the universes, the spaces, the skies, earths, waters, airs, illuminations, suns, stars, galaxies, worlds and bustling cities of all the worlds. Here I was again back to my own creation.

My dear disciple, I have seen many cycles of creation and dissolution. In your ignorance, you think much of this tiny cycle of your life which is nothing more than the turning upside down of a little mote in the beam of light. One turn, and you think this is your whole life and death. But ask me how many universes I have seen dissolved and created—and dissolved and created. Once upon a time there was an earth on which, for the entire duration, continuously, rain fell upon the earth, and each raindrop was the size of a pestle. Then I have seen an earth which blazed continuously and never cooled down. I have seen an earth around which ten suns blazed continuously and never cooled down. I have seen an earth on which people never, never learned to kindle a fire. I have seen an earth that was ruled by the ugliest and the most evil. I have seen dissolutions. I have seen entire creations wiped out by one wave of the sea. All the planets falling into each other I have seen. I have seen great cosmic conflagrations in which all our earths and planets were like so many cinders. And having seen it all, I see this changeability as nothing but a great melodrama taking place on one corner of the stage of consciousness. That consciousness which encompasses it all dwells in macrocosmic I-time.

Now take your mind from that vastness to a microscopic world.

Once upon a time the king of gods, Indra, was having a battle with another group of gods, and this first one, Indra, was defeated. Running for dear life, he wanted to find a place to hide. We all carry a body which is made up of our will. Remember this sentence: *We all carry a body which is made up of our will.* Dissociate the will, and the link with the physical nature of personality is broken. Your physical nature can then vanish. So the defeated Indra took his physical body (which was a projection of his spiritual will) and withdrew it into the core of his mind. He took his being, hid inside a mote and rested from the battle. He forgot all about the battles that were going on in the macroworld, as he was hiding in a microworld, and in that microworld he said, "Let me make a home." So he made for himself, through his will, a home, and began to live in it, and created for himself a lotus-shaped throne. With his will he created castles, palaces adorned with filigree work, etchings, murals in settings of jewels and pearls. He extended his consciousness and created within that mote a world; he made for himself a country to rule over—villages, cities, forests, gardens, rivers, smaller kings bowing at his feet, a sun and a moon and many stars. And again there were battles, politics, economics and the whole system. Eventually he died, leaving behind a son, then a grandson, O Rama. My disciple, in that mote I have seen the grandson of that Indra still ruling!

*Yoga-vasishtha, Nirvana Section II. 13*

You can go to the microscopic world. You can go to the macroscopic world. You can draw yourself to yourself, enter the core of your mind, and know that you are capable of creating all the universes there.

The finest vibration of a material energy-unit, not involving mental perception, may be said to take place in microcosmic It-time, whereas macrocosmic time extends through the duration of an entire mega-aeon *(mahakalpa)*. We shall define this later, but first we need to understand the relationship between microcosmic and macrocosmic time.

Ancient Indian seers saw a hierarchy of great beings of consciousness. They gave them names—Brahma, Vishnu, Shiva, Shakti. They knew that this universe runs in cycle, after cycle, after cycle. No yogi will say that God simply created the world. Instead, he will say that He creates the world, dissolves the world, and creates it again just as I sleep, I wake, I sleep and I wake again. Not that I shall die. I die; I am born; I die and I am reborn. There are wheels within wheels, cycles within cycles, times, space, sequences, awareness and many degrees of macroscopic and microscopic reality in between. Those levels of reality sometimes come in touch, and we have strange experiences. The yogis thought of the life span of a single creation, like this planet, to be 432 million years. (There are higher figures in other texts.) That duration was thought to be one single day of a Brahma, the lowest level of cosmic being. Multiply that by two, and you have a period of creation, then a period of dissolution. 864 million years is called a *kalpa*. That is one day and one night of a Brahma, a creating god. What for us is a period of 864 million years is one day and night in the consciousness of a being on the Brahma level. So one day and night thirty times would be a month; twelve times of that is one year; a hundred times that, a hundred years. That is, 36,000 cycles of creations and dissolutions of this one world is the life span of a Brahma, the lowest level of world-creating consciousness. There must be greater consciousness than that. A thousand times of that 36,000 cycles is one *ghatika* (2.5 hour) to Vishnu. There are sixty *ghatikas* in twenty four hours. So that is twenty four minutes to Vishnu! Multiply that by sixty, and this is one day and night to Vishnu; thirty days multiplied by twelve months times a hundred years—that is Vishnu's life span. A thousand times of that is one *pala* of Shiva's life. There are sixty *palas* in a *ghatika* (2.5 hours); multiply that by sixty again, and that's one *ghatika* to Shiva; multiply that by sixty and you have one day and night to Shiva. That, multiplied by thirty days times twelve months, times a hundred years is Shiva's life span. Shiva's life span multiplied by a thousand is a glance from the mother of the universe.

pala = 1/60 ghatika = 1/150 hour
ghatika = 2/5 hour (60 ghatikas = 24 hours)

Srsti, duration of a single creation (12 hours = 1/2 day)
   $4.32 \times 10^9$ years

Kalpa = 2 srstis, a cycle of creation and dissolution
   $8.64 \times 10^9$ years

lifespan = 100 years $\times$ 12 months $\times$ 30 days =
   $3.6 \times 10^4$ days

1 day to Brahma = 1 kalpa

Brahma's lifespan = $3.1104 \times 10^{14}$ years

1 ghatika to Vishnu = 1000 lifespans of Brahma =
   $3.1104 \times 10^{17}$ years

1 day to Vishnu = 60 ghatikas = $1.86624 \times 10^{19}$ years

Vishnu's lifespan = $6.718464 \times 10^{23}$ years

1 pala of Shiva's life = 1000 of Vishnu's lifespans =
   $6.718464 \times 10^{26}$ years

1 ghatika of Shiva's life = $4.0310784 \times 10^{28}$ years

1 day of Shiva's life = $2.41864704 \times 10^{30}$ years

Shiva's lifespan = $8.707129344 \times 10^{34}$ years

1 glance from the mother = 1000 of Shiva's lifespans =
   $8.707129344 \times 10^{37}$ years

It takes only one glance from the mother of the universe for us to attain enlightenment.

You can take that literally and lose heart, or you can take it at whatever level of reality it strikes you. That is the level of your consciousness, and you have to work from there. How long would it take us to attain enlightenment? How quickly can you gather the entire macroscopic world and center it into one mote, one tiny speck of the core of your consciousness? One glance from the mother of the universe is then condensed into a microscopic moment—microscopic I-time.

This all comes from what has been called in the ancient texts, the will, *sankalpa*. This universe is nothing but a play of your will. Who are you? You are the king of gods; you are Brahma, Vishnu and Shiva; you are the great angel, the archangel sitting on the right side of the throne of God.

The Upanishads state: *taj-jalan-iti shanta uapsita.* When an individual being is *shanta*, that is, when he has pacified all disturbances, then he worships that One and says *"taj-jalan*, from That I am born, in That I dwell, into That I dissolve back." A spark arises out of the fire, hovers around the fire, falls back into the fire. Sit by your household fire and name every spark, and see how long those sparks live! Or stand by the sea and name every bubble. All of three seconds is, for a big, beautiful, lovely bubble living all of three seconds, a long life. Our idea of time and space, of being small or large, changes as our consciousness grows. Remember when you were a child—how long it was from Christmas to Christmas? As we grow older the time passes more and more quickly. The year simply vanishes. As we grow in consciousness, that which was a long span of time seems very short. On the scale of a Brahma, a Vishnu, or a Shiva, on that scale of the great consciousness hierarchy, it is the same as the difference between a child's span from Christmas to Christmas compared to an adult's! To us, a glance from the mother's eyes (whew!) covers a vast period in cosmic time. But for Mother, it's nothing.

# Four

# God Within

Although philosophers, theologians, mystics and *bhakta* devotee-poets have all expressed their thoughts and feelings about God in many different ways, and however deeply we may have been moved by these writings, our lives go on as though we have understood nothing. It is difficult for the finite mind to grasp the infinite. Phrases like *God within* and *omnipresent* do not seem to make any impact on us. Lovers of God have often cried at their separation from Him, rejoiced in the promise of union, and have embraced with abandon anyone who remembered God—but do we? The light of love for God in the temple of the heart seems as though it is extinguished. In the visual concepts of God and in the visual descriptions of Him, our "normal" mind's notions find no anchor. God is strange, far away, above the white clouds, beyond the blue skies! Where? Where the spaceships travel? If God is above, are the astronauts of the future likely to photograph heaven and record the music of the angels?

We should remember that concepts such as that of God's being present somewhere above the yonder blue are not part of any valid theological system; they are mere folklore. All valid theologians have, instead, spoken of God as omnipresent—present everywhere. It is often said that Western man has difficulty grasping the idea of a God within, and those who take to the practice of meditation are often warned by their clergymen against relying on this idea. To these clergymen we say, "You have not understood the words of Christ, nor have you understood the Christian tradition. If God is omnipresent, that is, if He is present everywhere, at what point has He maliciously said to you, "Reverend Sir, though I dwell everywhere, I am so angered at your misrepresenting Me that I shall no longer dwell within you!" If God is everywhere, He is within the lips that open to utter the word *God*; She is within the faculty of speech from which the sound *God* proceeds; It is within the very mind where the thought of God occurs. And if I am in search of God, shall I go looking for Him in the places most distant from me or the ones closest to my soul?

Once upon a time a very poor widow lived in a village in India. She had no light in her hut; but there was a streetlight not far from her home. She barely eked out a livelihood by repairing the torn garments of the other village people. For this purpose she owned but a single needle.

One evening a kind young man was passing on the street and saw the old widow bending down under the streetlight frantically searching for something. Since it is customary in that country to address elderly persons by endearing and respectful terms such as "Mother," and to serve them, the young man approached the lady and asked her what she was searching for. She said, "My only needle is lost, and I cannot afford another. Perhaps you can help me find it, for your eyes are not as old and tired as mine."

The young man, too, looked for the needle under the street light but could not find it. At last he inquired, "are you certain, Mother, that this is where you lost the needle?"

"Oh, no," said she, "I lost the needle in my poor hut, but you see, young man, I have no lights in there!"

Only when the mind is in darkness do we go about looking for God under the street lights, as it were, of external objects—in churches, mosques, temples; in philosophies and theologies, in groups and clubs. When the mind is illuminated by the omnipresent light, we discover that the illumination has come from God within; the illumination is of God, from God, and in God. The process of opening the mind to that illumination is called meditation.

A little sponge, having heard much about a fathomless ocean, approached a wiser, older sponge and asked, "Teacher, where may I go to find the great, deep ocean?"

The larger sponge said, "Where will you go to find the ocean? The ocean fills both you and me. That which is within me and around me, that which is also within you and around you is the very fathomless ocean you are searching for." Thus does the all-pervading God fill us from within and permeate all that is around us.

Even though the idea of the omnipresence of God as the great living Self of the universe is difficult to grasp, we can begin to approach it by looking at our own little selves. Look at your own frame, wherever you are, sitting or standing. Within this frame can you imagine any part in which you are not present, where your life current is not? And just as your life current is the soul of your personality, so is the life force permeating the whole universe, the universal soul. It is omnipresent. In the whole universe there is no part where it is not. You might say that such an expanse is difficult to imagine, but that would also be the case with an ant that is crawling up an elephant's trunk; it would have difficulty imagining that from the trunk to the tail it is all one creature, with a single life unit pervading it all! Better still, let us refer to the parable of the two cells.

Once upon a time two blood cells in a person's body each developed into a genius. One became an inspired mystic and philosopher while the other chose to be a cynical scientist. The blood cell that had become a mystic stood by the walls of an artery and announced, "Fellow cells, harken! I must share with you a great vision I have been granted. We are not all apart, each cell having a separate life of its own. There is a great omnipresent being whose life force we share, from whom we are born, in whom we dwell, and into whom we each finally dissolve. Though the individual cell may die, life continues in that great being. That great one is so vast that billions of us all cannot fathom his greatness. None of us can comprehend all his thoughts, knowledge and action. That being is called *man.*"

The blood cell that had become a scientist scowled and jeered and taunted, challenging the mystic, and saying: "What a visionary you are, talking without proof! *Where* is this great being you call *man*? Look around you, fellow cells, do you see any such being? Mr. Mystic, can you show us this man?"

Is there any way that the blood cells in that artery could see man? Could they imagine human activities such as writing this book or reading it? But even though each cell has a little life of its own, they all share collectively, by a thread unknown to them, in the life force of the person in whom they are joined. So it is with our individual lives in God. The person's life force, as experienced by the blood cell, is neither male nor female. Similarly, any attempt to attribute a gender to God reflects an abysmal ignorance. All that is masculine or feminine in the universe is from that one. The same applies to the question of whether God is one or many. God cannot be one, for one is a number, and God is not to be numbered for She is infinite. The relation of the manifold objects with God is the same as that of numbers with infinity. When we add $5 + 5$ the result is $10$; add $10 + 5$, we get $15$, which is larger than $10$. But if we add $\infty + 5$ do we get $\infty 5$? Or from $\infty + 10$ do we get $\infty 10$? Both times, all we get is $\infty$. Is $\infty + 5 = \infty$ a smaller infinity than $\infty + 10 = \infty$? Infinity neither increases by additions to it nor decreases by subtractions from it. When so many waves rise in the ocean, does the ocean itself increase? When the waves subside, does the ocean become smaller? All the objects and life-units in the universe are as though waves of numbers arising from the ocean of infinity; they do not dwell apart from infinity, and they finally merge into it. To repeat, we are like numbers, and God is infinity. How ludicrous for the wave to resist the ocean; how pitiful for the little number to try to remain apart in the face of infinity. It is as though the bubble on the wave's bosom were to boast, "See what a mighty bubble am I—how large, all of a third of an inch across—and enjoying the longevity of four full seconds. I wish to remain myself and not be lost in some fathomless ocean!"

Are there many gods? How can there be? If I move my right arm in circles, how many movements do you see?

One. Now I also move my left arm. Are there two motions? Yes. Yet it's only me! How many suns, moons, stars, and how many powers there are, but God says, "Child, it's only I!" Much as the same ocean is a wave, a tide, a bay, sea, gulf, and the shallow wash on a beach, much as a person's life force becomes uncountable myriad changes of life force in so many blood cells, so does one infinite become many in the universe. As we are each the ruling spirits of our individual personalities, so are all the gods and deities the ruling spiritual energies of the natural bodies and forces in the universe. They, too, are grand souls, subject to the laws of *karma*.

In this context the followers of a given incarnation of God, such as Christ or Krishna, are likely to ask about the place of these incarnations in the yoga view of God. The idea that God becomes flesh has been well known for thousands of years in the yoga tradition. It is emphatically stated in the Bhagavad Gita:

> Whenever there is decline of virtue and the rise of evil,
> I send myself forth.
> For the protection of the good,
> For the destruction of evil,
> To re-establish virtue,
> I am born from aeon to aeon.
> *Bhagavad Gita IV. 8*

Elsewhere it is said that there have been many more than just one incarnation in history, that such incarnations repeatedly occur. The word used for this is *avatara*, a descendent. God's power and manifestation descend from time to time, from place to place, in civilization after civilization, from planet to planet, speaking many languages and wearing many garments in order to fulfill the missions the particular times and places require. "There are as many universes as there are hairs on the body of God," says one ancient text, for God, in Her unbounded compassion, must incarnate in all those worlds, as He must also at different times on our own planet. We paraphrase from the *Mahabharata:*

> When I am born among the *yakshas*, I look, speak, dress and behave like a *yaksha*. When I am born among the *gandharvas* or the *devas*, I look, speak, dress and behave just like them. No one there knows me apart from the people of that world.
>
> This time I am born among human beings to fulfill a certain mission, and only a few know my true divine nature.
> *Mahabharata, Ashvamedha-parvan, Anu-gita 54. 14-20*

The Bhagavad Gita clarifies, "the naive, seeing me in a human form, mistake me for being a human, not knowing my supreme, transcendent nature as the great Lord." The question arises, How do we know the true incarnation from a false one? Has not the Lord said in the Gospels, "I am *the* way, the light and the life?"

The yogi answers, "Indeed!" The Lord has said this repeatedly, whenever He has appeared. We read in the Gita: "Whatever there is glorious, powerful, great, know that to be an emanation only from my nature" X.41.

Whose are these utterances? Does Jesus contradict Krishna, or vice versa? As the yogi sees it, both manifestations of the same Lord utter the same declaration, descending into humanity to remind us of this truth from time to time. We hear from the Krishna incarnation in the Gita,

> On whatever path people walk, they come unto me.
> Whatever form or aspect of mine they worship,
> Toward that very aspect I strengthen their faith;
> And through that faith they come unto me.
> *Bhagavad Gita IV. 11; VII, 21-22.*

Believing these declarations to be true, the yogi,

teaching in whatever land or civilization, strengthens
people's faith towards whatever incarnation they accept.
In the Christian countries yogis have thus brought the true
meaning of Christian worship to the hearts of thousands.
After they had learned to meditate, for instance, many
who had quit their churches begin to attend them again
with a renewed faith, and many who had rejected the
mass and other forms of worship began to receive the
joy of participation again. Now they hear the voice of God
within, giving a new meaning to worship. The yogi minis-
ters to the people of all faiths, everywhere, and lets them
see their beloved ever-present God in their own church,
temple, mosque, pyramid or pagoda; but first they see Him
in the temple that is the human personality.

This still leaves the strict believer of any given faith in
a quandary. For if his credo states that X is the only true
incarnation and that all the others are false gods, then how
can such a believer accept other incarnations as true? The
answer to this comes from *bhakti* yoga, the yoga of
devotion: Whatever incarnation or face of the Lord you
have accepted, be true to that one. Sing of him; speak of
him; carry the good news of that one alone. But let others
do the same also. There is your deliverance. (At some
point this *saguna bhakti*, devotion to God in a form, will
lead you to *nirguna*, the formless, from whose infinity all
incarnations descend and into whom all their qualified
quanta merge.)

Mankind has always accepted the idea of the many
faces of God. People of every race believe Him to look like
themselves. The Buddhas of the Gangetic Valley are
Indian, in Gandhara art they are Greek, in Tibet, Tibetan,
in Japan, Japanese. Even the name undergoes a change.
In Japan the Buddha is Butsu. The same thing has

happened to Yeshua who is, in Latin, Jesus. In China, he looks Chinese. In a Japanese manger scene all the figures are Japanese. In Europe and America Jesus is European (he is not even Jewish). In an Indian Christmas card Mary wears a *sari*. Perhaps modern American youth will some day dress Jesus in levis—but God wears neither toga, nor kimono, nor blue jeans.

The voice of God is heard differently in different centuries. It is like the voice of an orator who is speaking into a single microphone, with people listening to many loudspeakers in different rooms, or over many radio receivers. Each separate loudspeaker or radio receiver says, "Listen to me," and an ignorant person might place his own receiver on an altar, and revere it, and condemn everyone else's receiver as a false god! This is what the claimants of all religions have done when the voice of God has been heard in different centuries, different civilizations and through other incarnations. To the followers of each incarnation God has promised, "I shall return." Yet when he does return we reject him—again and again. In ancient India God spoke Sanskrit; in Israel, Aramaic; in Arabia, Arabic; in the Europe of the Middle Ages, Latin; today we think God speaks only American English! All else is alien, false—something to be rejected. We can never reach the true realization of God through such narrow views. The Vedas, on the other hand, say that

> A thousand heads has that Great Person,
> A thousand eyes, a thousand feet;
> Permeating the entire earth from all sides
> He transcends the span of the ten fingers (dimensions).
> *Rig Veda X.90.1*

Another question common to all systems of theology has to do with the question of the humanity versus the divinity of an incarnation. A major split occurred in Christianity between the Western churches in which it was believed that both humanity and divinity were united in the person of Christ, whereas the Eastern churches accepted only the divinity of Christ. The problem is solved in Vedanta by the assertion that God may incarnate only in partial glory. So in a way we all are "God become flesh," for all life is God. We are *amshavataras*, partial incarnations; however infinitesimal, a spark of God is in us. In fact, the Kashmir version of the famous verse from the Bhagavad Gita reads: "Whenever there is a decline of virtue and the rise of evil, I send a portion of myself forth." Not all incarnations are equal in their degrees of divinity, or humanity. What their proportion is depends on how many *kalas*, cosmic powers of God, are to be made manifest for the fulfulment of a specific mission. Thus, the duality between the human and the divine nature is easily observed in any given incarnation. Jesus cursing the fig tree or crying out on the cross, "Father, Father, why hast thou abandoned me?" certainly seems to manifest the human aspect of the incarnation. When speared in the side, does he not bleed? Does he not suffer physical pain? But then the divine spirit asserts its presence and will rise again. In the words of Swami Rama, "Jesus suffered, but Christ did not suffer."

There are many types of incarnations. God becomes the universe; God becomes flesh; God may also make His *shakti* (power and glory) manifest through someone who was born human and who has, through the practice of yoga, managed to obey the command, "Be ye perfect as our Father who is in heaven is perfect." Such a human-seeming person is called a *siddha*—literally, a perfected one. The difference between an incarnation and a *siddha*

is that in the former, the divinity has descended into
humanity whereas in the latter, humanity has ascended to
divinity. The descent and/or the ascent having taken place,
the two, *avatara* and *siddha*, no longer differ from one
another in nature. In the tradition that recognizes and
reveres such divinity, both the *avataras* and the *siddhas* are
addressed as the Lord, *Bhagavan*:

> All mastery, virtue (and universal law and order),
> Fame, glory, knowledge and dispassion—
> These six are termed *bhaga*. One endowed with these
> Is the Lord, *Bhagavan*.

The powers and acts of the Lord are uncountable. It is
common in India to recite in worship a thousand names of
the Lord, each name denoting or connoting a power or an
act, and there are many such collections of "thousand-
names" in which each *mantra* in the collection ends with
*namas*, meaning, "Homage, honor, surrender to Thee; I
renounce all my claims to ego." Having thus made a
thousand prostrations the devotee goes on to state, "I
cease here not because of a limit to thy names, but for the
end of my own capacity." There is no limit to the names
of God because all names are the names of God, and in all
things God is incarnate. It is tragic that all-God *(sarvesh-
vara)*, the all-spirit *(sarvatman)*, the God of all has been
divided up among churches, religions and nations, each
having snatched up a portion of the divine grace and glory
and claiming to possess exclusively all glory. Nations at
war each hoist a flag and claim the divine right to conquer,
and the bishops of each side bless the warriors in the name
of the same God. The followers of two opposing cults
face each other across a street, each condemning the other.
They both have a common litany, "My God is the true
God; yours is the false one!" In the modern intellectual

theology *Theos* (Greek for *God*) is sacrificed for the benefit of *logia*, intellectual acrobatics. Even though many Vedanta texts, over twelve centuries, are filled with similar polemic, one difference remains; they constantly remind the seeker to merge logic into contemplation and thereby to know God directly.

The differences in theologies arise because those who do not *know* God make statements about His nature by guesswork alone, often attributing to Him their personal subconscious leanings. The original prophet, or founding saint, of every religion had inner knowledge and a clear vision, but the disciples, not having had the direct perception, could only guess at the meaning of the master's words. Soon each of the proverbial blind men, each defining an elephant in his own way, established his own following.

Because none of the statements articulated about God can fully apply, the philosophers of true realization have chosen silence. If they must speak they state simply, "None of these." So said the Upanishads; so said Meister Eckhart. The Buddhists, who are often accused of being atheists, define the ultimate reality as *shunya*, which is not the relative nihil of our simple limited wordly cognition. We paraphrase Nagarjuna, who was the codifier of the formal Buddhist philosophy in the first century A.D., and his commentator Chandrakirti:

> The four possible categories, *kotis*, of statement about any facet of reality are:
> It is thus,
> It is not thus,
> It both is and is not thus,
> It neither is nor is not thus.
> The ultimate reality, *shunya*, is none of these.

So, *Tathagata-garbha*, the womb of the thus-come, the

ultimate of suchness (positive) is that nihil which is not
simply the negation of an existing reality—it is in the same
breath the negation of that negation, too. So where does
that leave us as far as a definition of God is concerned?
Back to the drawing board of personal experience.

It is because the founding philosophers of all religions
had received the personal experience of God that we can
trace a common thread of unity running through many
divergent systems. Let us try to compare some of these
views.

In the yoga-Vedanta tradition God is seen on three
levels of reality:

| | |
|---|---|
| *Brahman:* | the transcendental, absolute, transpersonal being |
| *Hiranya-garbha:* | the golden womb; God, the imma-nent spirit of the universe |
| or | or |
| *Ishvara:* | the Lord; the personal God |
| *Avatara:* | the incarnate being, such as Jesus or Krishna, manifest in history |

The Buddhist philosophers, having made the basic
definition of the ultimate reality as *shunya*, defined above,
went on to see the same reality on two levels:

| | |
|---|---|
| *Paramartha satya:* | the supreme, transcendental truth |
| *Samvrti satya:* | the veiled, relative truth as seen in the universe |

They saw the Buddha's rulership over these levels of reality
in categories analogous to the Brahman-Ishvara-Avatara
triad of yoga-Vedanta. For instance, the Buddhist perception of the Buddha triad is as follows:

| *Dharma-kaya:* | the transcendental, transpersonal being (analogous to Brahman) |
| *Sambhoga-kaya:* | the enlightened universal spirit immanent in the universe |
| *Nirmana-kaya:* | the historical Buddhas who incarnate from time to time |

In Christianity we see the same threefold analog in the Father, the Son and the Holy Ghost. Let us look at it again:

| Yoga-Vedanta | Buddhist | Christian |
|---|---|---|
| Brahman | Dharma-kaya | God, the Father Logos, the transcendent reality |
| Hiranya-garbha or Ishvara | Sambhoga-kaya | Holy Ghost, the teaching spirit in the universe |
| Avatara | Nirmana-kaya | Son, God in history |

It is the same God. It is the same God. It is the same God. We have no doubt that in other traditions similar analogs will be found, even if the details of the philosophy are not always fully developed. Similarities between religions are shared in many other areas as well. For example, the yoga tradition includes the many *siddhas*; the Buddhists speak of the *arhants*; the Christians pray for the intercession of the saints. Even though it might appear that hard-lining theologians of each faith refuse to acknowledge the sanctity of the saints of other faiths, those who are wiser and more spiritually realized do not hold such a narrow view. In India a liberal syncretism has developed to its fullest possible extent. For example, read this poem with which Shudraka, one of the most ancient Sanskrit playwrights, and a devotee of Shiva (the deity dormant in us), begins his drama, *The Little Clay Cart:*

> Knees folded and feet knotted with a double coil
>   of his snake *(kundalini),*
>
> His senses suspended, as all perceptions have ceased
>   through retention of the vital breath within,
>   and all processes withdrawn,
>
> As he, with his vision of truth, sees the
>   identity of self with the Self—
>
> May Shiva's *samadhi* of total absorption
>   in Brahman
>   caused by the revelations of *shunya,*
>
> Protect you (the audience).*

Brahman—the transcendent, *atman*—the self, Shiva—a manifestation of the personal God, as well as the Buddhist great nihil *(shunya)* all fit here within a single system of thought. Such is the beauty of a pure mind that it sees all facets of truth, all levels of reality, within a single, perfect, infinite whole—denying none, accepting all without prejudice. For this reason, in a very popular prayer in the Upanishads, one asks for the blessing of one who is *a-nira-karishnu,* one who does not deny, who does not negate, who does not refute, does not exclude, does not contradict, does not say, No. When a student is first ordained he is also advised to be *a-nirakarishnu,* for it is the nature of both a seeker and a saint that they always accept and accommodate.

But many of those who practice yoga in the West are

---

* Usharbudh Arya, "Man in Kavya," *Literature East and West* (April, 1972), pp. 183-208.

not concerned with these matters. Instead, some of their most important questions are in this area:

> I practice yoga for its intrinsic benefits. Is it necessary for me to accept your explanation of God?

> I am a Christian; I accept Christ alone as my savior; I practice meditation to deepen my prayer; I do not wish to be untrue to the doctrine that is taught to me by my church. Must I replace my doctrine with yours?

> I am an atheist or agnostic; I have no interest in God, but I enjoy meditation. How far can your philosophy of God accommodate my convictions?

Yoga is not a religion or a church. It requires no belief in a doctrine, no credo. All yoga philosophy is concerned with the experience of meditation and nothing else. It does not require anyone to adhere to a belief system. It does advise one to practice the scientific and time tested method of meditation, the efficacy of which is so well proved that the followers of any religion or philosophy, who have come into contact with yoga, have attempted to incorporate it into their own system. All the paths in India, China, Tibet, Nepal, Mongolia, Shri Lanka, Burma, Thailand, Laos, Cambodia, Vietnam, Indonesia and Japan, which includes hundreds of systems of philosophy and faith developed over four thousand years, have accepted yoga methods to varying degrees and in one way or another. Among the Muslims many Sufis have established an accord with yoga. Western contact with yoga goes back at least to the fourth century B.C. when Alexander, the invader from Macedonia, brought Greek armies to India, and there are many indications of the influence of yoga in the history of Christian nations. The current trend to rediscover the contemplative tradition within Christianity has also produced many writings on what has become known as Christian yoga. A qualified teacher can therefore teach the methods of meditation within the context of a Christian—or Jewish—prayer. So there is Hindu yoga, Buddhist yoga or Christian yoga, but the yoga tradition proper requires no adherence to any of these belief systems. In a religion one is asked to believe first and practice later; in yoga one simply practices the methods and waits for the doctrine to develop out of the experience. Meditation is the laboratory work involved when one is seeking after God. You do not enter a physics lab, either believing or disbelieving the *sutra*, "water is $H_2O$." You follow your professors' instructions and prove the formula, yourself, through methodical experiment.

To one who does not believe in God, we advise the practice of yoga for such personal benefits as health and well being, freedom from tension and stress, emotional equilibrium and general strength of character—all this comes without any reference to God. We assure the scientist that the practice of meditation will clear his mind so that intuitive flashes regarding the mysteries of nature will appear. The prayer-minded among them will go to deeper, silent prayer. A poet or an artist will find instant and inspired creativity through yoga. A philosopher may test, through meditation, the hypotheses presented by transcendentalist philosophers like Socrates and Kant. And as the mind develops clarity, equilibrium, harmony and intuitive faculties, questions begin to arise regarding the subtler meanings of the purpose and modes of life. One begins to suspect that a conscious reality exists beyond the shallower surfaces of the mind—something unfamiliar beyond the familiar, perhaps infinite beyond the finite. At some time during meditation one comes to a state of ineffable tranquility and feels as if he has touched the fringes of infinity. Only then do some begin to believe in a transcendental reality. If you are allergic to outdated words like God, call the source of your experience the factor X.

Among the seekers after God, however, there are those who ask, "Do I attain the knowledge of God by my methodical yoga effort alone? Can I not simply accept my savior and surrender to His grace?" The answer to this question can be found only through a sound study of the psychology of spiritual growth. How can we prevent the "satanic" ego from coming in the way of our surrender? The yoga tradition says, Purify yourself and the grace will flow. If you walk two steps towards God, His grace will take four steps towards you. The method of yoga simply removes the hindrances from your side by purifying the body and mind. (This, of course, applies only to those who are seeking grace. For those who wish to go only as far as bodily health and mental relaxation through yoga, but no further, we reassert—no doctrinal belief is necessary.) The principle of an ever-present grace that flows towards us when we remove the hindrances is fundamental to the yoga tradition, however. This grace flows from the God within us. It is the God within who calls us to prayer and to meditation; he calls, calls and ever calls—and we respond. You are reading this book because the call became strong and clear enough for you. It is not that the call was weaker before; it was only that your inner ear had gone out of tune. Gradually it becomes attuned, and you have chosen to read this book rather than watch "Wonder Woman" on TV. The sage-philosopher, Vidyaranya says, "If you want to hear the voice of your boy in the choir, you have to quiet the voices of other singers." Yoga is the process of that quieting.

The presence of God within is called the *kundalini*, the *shakti*, the *potentia*, of God within us. It is a ray of light, life, conscious—because of which we know, "I am." It is as though God has become flesh in each of us by projecting a however-minute ray of His being into the physical person. It makes us into part-incarnations of God. This minute ray is said to be subtle and slim; for want of a better analogy, it is said to be like one ten-thousandth of a hair's breadth. It shines like a flash of lightning with the light of ten thousand suns. It is the candle burning in the temple of God which is our body, our personality. This divine energy constitutes the force-field of life around which our bodies are built. Take a magnet; place on it a piece of paper on which you have sprinkled some iron filings, and these filings arrange themselves around the pattern of the magnetic force-field. Thus is the human body, in all its symmetry and harmony, arranged along the 325,000 energy currents emanating from the *kundalini*. Thus is the human personality created in the divine image.

All our life, power, creativity, thoughts, feelings, emotions, sensations, derive their energy from the sparks of *kundalini*. All that mankind has ever experienced, expressed or created—poetry, literature, pyramids, peace, war, diplomacy, history, medicine and galaxies of books— are minor releases of this same energy. All that goes on within us, mentally or physically, is a series of implosions from this force. All that is perfect, good and healthy derives from its purity; all that is imperfect, evil or un- healthy is because the energy released from *kundalini* became warped through the non-conductive impediments we have created.

The *kundalini* comprises all of consciousness and all of life within; its life-force projects two other fields of force to run the human personality. The first is the mind-field to which its consciousness imparts a semblance of awareness. The second is the *prana*-, or the vitality-field of our personality, to which it imparts the semblance of aliveness. The points at which these fields receive, from the *kundalini*, the requisite sparks to effect the psychophysiological operations of the personality are called the *chakras*, and the "quantum" of energy required for such operability is extremely minute.

The tradition asserts, however, that the true power of *kundalini* is lying dormant in us. God's energy dormant? Not within itself, for in all of our impulses it is that which is calling us inward. Let us revert to the tradition and call it by the pronoun appropriate for the mother of all our divine nature—she. In all our energy impulses, in all our implosions she is calling us towards herself. It is we who are dormant—asleep to her call.

As we purify ourselves gradually, the sanctifying force of the *kundalini*, the divine ray, takes over more and more of our life, and we learn to walk in God. We may change the famous devotional hymn by one word:

> He walks *in* me and He talks *in* me
> And He tells me I am His own;
> And the joys we share
> As we tarry there
> None other has ever known.

The *kundalini* contains the divine light and sound. In the meditative, or mystic, experience light is projected more and more unhindered, and that is why, in all religions, a vision of light is equated with the presence of God. (The divine sound, *mantra*, also becomes a pure vibration and leads us inward.)

If we fail to heed the inner call the *kundalini* becomes

the fallen snake, dwelling in the lowest centers, and it then becomes the ruling force of the subterranean regions of darkness, far below any experience even of the lowest of the seven *chakras*, the seven heavens. But when she ascends in her fullness through the seven heavens, the seven churches, the seven lotuses, the seven *chakras*, finally the portals of the seventh heaven open and the thousand-petaled lotus blooms—the sun of the thousand rays shines in full splendor. This is the nature of God within who is *not only within* but also in all things and beyond them.

This is no vision, no momentary experience, for thereafter one's spirit dwells in the great infinite Self. There are no words to describe this state of superconsciousness. Take the light from the hearts of ten thousand suns and condense it into the core of a diamond. Empty the intergalactic spaces of all particles and planets and fill them with liquid light in which each drop is the core of that diamond—each drop contains the light of ten thousand suns! *It is a living light imbued with God's own Self-awareness.* If you pick up a person and throw him into that cosmic ocean of liquid light at an incredible depth, the light is of such intensity and is so infused into the subtlest consciousness of the person, that from that moment on the person is no more; only the living light declares, "I am that I am. The splendor that shines in the sun, that person I am." When this living light touched Saul on the way to Damascus, he could not open his eyes for three days afterwards.

Such a touch of light cannot occur by one's effort alone. It is the *guru* who has himself become the vehicle for this light, through whom the great being flows unhindered, whose mental touch lifts the consciousness of a qualified disciple and elevates it to the fullest awareness described above. Grace is, thus, not simply a speculation about an ephemeral idea; it becomes real in terms of the *kundalini*. The *guru*, a vehicle of God, touches his own fully awake *kundalini* to the disciple's dormant one and awakens him. Only one who is capable of imparting such grace is called a *guru* in the yoga tradition, for *guru* is not a person; only the light of God flowing freely through the person is the *guru*. The first *guru* is hiranya-garbha, the golden womb of the universe, the holy spirit with whom we become linked by the *guru's* grace.

But until we remove the bondage and taints of false ego from the freedom of our spiritual volition are we qualified for such grace. Only when we can say, "Thy will be done," do we become the vehicles of His will. God, as understood by the yogi, shall continue to call upon this little wave, this little individual will, but shall not impose His supreme volition on it. The first steps in meditation begin to reduce the ego that impedes the full opening of our own divine will, and when we reach the highest possible nameless, we may name it God, or whatever else, in futile attempts at describing it to others. We may write a million tomes of theology, dissecting every hair of "God," but, alas, no one will understand—till the experience itself dawns on him.

Seek that, Friend.

# Five

# The Schema of Creation

Because we all begin with a bias in favor of or against certain views, there is much confusion about the differences and similarities between Eastern and Western schools of philosophy. We take an opinion with which we agree and compare it with something that comes from the background of another school of thought. We do not understand it, and so it seems disagreeable to us. This is especially the case when modern Western writers try to compare Western philosophy with Eastern systems. They say, for instance, "We believe in a transcendental God; they believe in a personal God." This is a gross oversimplification, for Indian philosophy is not one single homogeneous system. It is the result of over four thousand years of growth in an area equal to the size of Europe (excluding the U.S.S.R.) in a nation where philosophical speculation is the favorite pastime of almost everybody. The philosophical systems in Europe developed over a shorter period (that of approximately twenty-six centuries since the time of Pythagoras), but it is still not possible to make generalized statements about what European philosophy believes in (or disagrees with) because there are so many varying hypotheses and views to be examined, rejected or accepted. This is exactly the case with Indian philosophy. There is, in fact, no belief that has ever been propounded in the Western philosophical and theological systems that has not been similarly examined, accepted or refuted by some Indian philosopher. What is more, each system of Indian philosophy represents an attempt to develop its own cosmology, philosophy of God, and theory of creation. One attitude in India seems to be unique, however, and that is the fact that many thinkers, especially those who have become popular among the general masses, have diligently attempted to develop a syncretic, or common, philosophy, drawing from all the various systems, and trying to find a synthesis.

In this chapter we will follow that tradition; we will look into two schools—Vedanta and Sankhya—and see how the systems developed in each fit together to provide a complete schema. Vedanta is known as, "the end of wisdom." This school, as we have stated earlier, is monistic; it postulates only one single substratum of reality— Brahman. However, at the empirical, or practical, level it does not deny the relative realities. The other school, known as Sankhya, is dualistic; it postulates the eternally separated, mutually interdependent conscious principle *(purusha)* and the principle of unconscious matter, or nature *(prakriti)*. Then a great body of texts, called the Puranas, consisting of many millions of verses, synthesizes these two systems and finds a place for many divergent principles in one single scheme. In order for us to understand God in creation it is necessary to define briefly the various categories of this synthesized system.

The highest word expressing God is Om, the only word in any language that is totally genderless and without declension of any kind. No kind of alteration to this word is possible, for Om signifies that immutable principle which is nameless and formless, the superconscious which never undergoes any change. A detailed explanation of this transcosmic sound and what it signifies, is to be found in the *Mandukya Upanishad*. Only seventeen verses long, and covering a single page, it includes the commentary by Gaudapada (the *guru* of the *guru* of the great *guru*, Shankaracharya) which is difficult to interpret in itself. There are a number of authentic translations available in English, however, which may convey some of the basic precepts.*

The Upanishads record the ancient dialogues between the great masters and their very close disciples between the fifteenth and the fifth centuries B.C. Then, in the eighth century A.D., their philosophy was further systematized and developed into a formal school, called Vedanta, by the great Shankaracharya. According to this philosophy, Om is undefinable to the degree that even the statement that Om is undefinable is considered to be an attempt at definition, for the moment we make this statement we are no longer in the realm of Om but are making a formal statement. Therefore, so as not to delude ourselves into thinking that by talking of Om we are raising our consciousness to infinity, we use the word *Brahman*.

---

*    The reader may begin his study of this Upanishad in Sarvepali Radhakrishnan and Charles A. Moore, eds., *A Source Book in Indian Philosophy* (Princeton: Princeton University Press, 1957), pp. 55-56. From there one may proceed with research in one of the numerous translations available. These will be found listed in various bibliographies on Indian philosophy and under "Upanishads" in most public libraries.

The fundamental statement about Brahman is simply *sat-chit-ananda*, existence-consciousness-bliss. Brahman is not collective existence or consciousness of joy. It is not the sum total of all existence, consciousness or pleasure. *Sat-chit-ananda* is not a statement of qualities or attributes, for Brahman is non-qualitative, without attributes. Existence, consciousness and bliss is the very nature of Brahman. In other words, that *is* Brahman. Existence, but not the existence of an object or a person, nor existence as opposed to an absence of this or that; consciousness, but not that of a delimited being, not opposed to an unconscious state or principle nor in any way related to higher or lower degrees of consciousness; bliss, but without the opposition, or relationship, between pain and pleasure —this is Brahman. In Brahman as existence-consciousness-bliss, the universe and its phenomena have not yet begun to be diversified. This Brahman is *nir-guna*, without qualification, without delimitation, yet all *shakti*, *potentia* is within Brahman, one with Brahman.

The *shakti*, all-potency, in Brahman is threefold: *iccha, jnana, kriya*—will, knowledge and action. It is interesting to note that the Latin word *potentia*, from which the English word potency is derived, comes from *poteo*, meaning, *I can*, and when we use it in connection with Brahman, it implies the Brahman's omnipotence, capacity, capability. This term was repeatedly used by St. Thomas Aquinas when he first formalized Christian theology, and it implies not only capability, but also the knowledge of that capability. The Sanskrit word, *shakti*, has the same kind of source. It is derived from the root *shak* which also means, *I can*, and it is in this knowledge that all knowledge is included. For instance, Brahman's will and knowledge are not separated from Its action. The word Brahman is neuter (not feminine or masculine), but all principles dwell within Brahman, and the words *shakti* and *potentia* are both feminine. At this stage the masculine principle had not yet developed.

The question is often raised, Why did God create the universe? Why does He produce these many phenomena? Why go into all the trouble? The simple answer is that being implies a nature, a certain potency, but potency not used, not manifested nor projected, is no potency at all. The statement, "I can" simply means, "I know, I will (it), and I do." If you ask the ocean why it goes to the trouble of creating waves, the ocean simply replies, "It is no trouble at all!" Ask the fire why it produces flames, and the fire says, "I *am* all the flames." It is in this sense that the entire universe is said to be in Brahman, rises from Brahman like numbers from infinity, dwells in Brahman, *is* Brahman, returns to Brahman.

We have already spoken of *maya*, the innate power of Brahman, and it needs very little further comment here except to say that when the *omni-potentia, sarva-shakti,* of Brahman remains unmanifest there is no scope for *maya*. The ancient texts state that creativity is a negative function. We can understand this by way of an illustration. Take a block of marble. How many pieces of sculpture lie dormant, unmanifested, in that single block? There is no count. By simply stretching one's imagination into the block one may see the busts of a million statesmen, philosophers, saints or whatever else we may choose to perceive. An artist is commissioned to produce one specific bust, so with his hammer and chisel, he chisels away and unveils the specific bust that is required of him. But in that process he must negate millions of other possible busts. His act of negation is more emphatic than his creativity, but the creativity is an illustration of the statement, "I can," even though it is unspecified. The function of *maya* is to bring the specifics from the unmanifest into manifestation, and in so doing *maya* must use two special powers known as *avarana-shakti* and *vikshepa-shakti*—the power to veil and the power to project. In other words, in order for the artist to project, to manifest, that one single bust, the power to veil a million others is implied. One cannot function without the other. At this point the positive and the negative aspects of all things yet to come are brought into polarization, and the rest of creation is the interaction between these two realities. All interaction in the universe is between the polarities of these two.

If it were not for the veiling power of *maya* all the manifest energies, *shaktis*, of Brahman could become manifest simultaneously in equal degree, thus canceling each other out. In other words, if all manifestation took place, no manifestation would take place. This brings to our attention the problems of evil and imperfection in the universe. How can the perfect God create an imperfect world? Since God is good, He cannot create evil. Indeed, we would agree. However, the perfection in God implies His infinity, and the words *finite* and *perfect* are mutually contradictory. The Vedas explain perfection in the words used by philosophers and mathematicians to define infinity:

> *Purnam adah purnam idam*
> *Purnat purnam udachyate.*
> *Purnasya purnam adaya*
> *Purnam evavashishyate.*

> That is perfect, this is perfect,
> Perfect is taken from the perfect;
> Upon taking the perfect from the perfect,
> What remains is only perfect.

If the sculptor tries to create all possible busts out of a single block of marble, there would be no creation. Creation means that specific powers of God are projected into *finite* spaces and times. Creation cannot be both perfect and finite; if it could, the powers, *shaktis, potentiae,* might as well remain unmanifest within the perfect being. Trying to project them all, in equal perfection, into all-space and all-time constitutes not creation, but dissolution, of the universe, for the finite specificity of the phenomena is inherent in the process of creation. Evil exists only in relativity, in the relationship among the finite specifics within creation. Where relativity is dissolved into the substratum of perfection, there is not even a dream of evil.

In another tradition it is stated that the mother of the universe conducts five operations: *srishti*—creation, *sthiti*—preservation, *samhriti*—dissolution, *tirodhana*—veiling, conceiling, and *anugraha*—compassionate Grace. It is by veiling some of her powers that she creates—only by negating many can she project a specific one—and what she creates, she may preserve or dissolve (take back to her bosom). From some, her perfection is thus veiled, but others who truly seek are compassionately graced by the vision of her true nature.

The Vedanta philosophy considers *ajnana*, ignorance, to be forever inherent among the powers of God. As an analogy, God may be compared to a person of great intelligence who has mastery of many fields of learning. When he is solving a great mathematical problem, his poetry is at that point dormant, asleep; he wills himself to remain, as it were, ignorant of his poetic ability and chooses not to bring it to manifestation. Not that he is truly ignorant; he has selected, for a given time and space, to manifest only his mathematical expertise. God has such will that he can thus delimit His manifestation. If God willed His perfection—infinity—to be at that very imperfect time and limited space where God wills and knows the sun to be, then immediately the sun would cease to be the sun and would merge, dissolve, into infinity. For the sun to remain the sun, it has to be in imperfect space-time relativity. This is similarly true of every vibration in the universe (and everything in the universe ultimately reduces to a vibration), whether that of an unconscious photon or a conscious soul. Call this necessary imperfection of relationships among these phenomena to be evil if that is your choice of terms; evil is the imperfect relationship among the imperfect phenomena.

Where we use the term *ajnana*, ignorance, in this writing, the term must be understood in this very technical and well-defined philosophical sense. It does not postulate an ignorant God—rather, it postulates God's power to veil his perfect all-knowledge and omniscience so that specific delimited knowledge relative to specific time and space may be brought into manifestation, just as the sculptor chooses to unveil one particular bust from the block of marble.

At this point *maya* diverges into two channels, the *atman* principle, or the conscious individuations, and the un-*atman* principle, the non-self, unconscious, material nature—termed, respectively, in the Sankhya philosophy, *purusha* and *prakriti*. Many texts such as the Bhagavad Gita even use the words *maya* and *prakriti* interchangeably. The rest of the schema, from here on, is more or less identical in both the Vedanta and the Sankhya systems because the duality has already occurred, the polarities are beginning to interact.

Let us now examine the categories in the processes of conscious individuation, and here we deal with the personalization of the transpersonal. The name for the personal God is *Ishvara*, the Lord, who operates at three levels:

> *Karana Ishvara*: God, the cause; beyond the universe
> *Hiranya-garbha Ishvara:* the golden womb; God in the universe
> *Virat Ishvara:* God of the universe, whose body is the universe

The first of these, the *Karana Ishvara,* is analogous to the Judeo-Christian concept of God beyond the universe. Here the *maya* of Brahman has already determined that the unmanifest Self comes to be manifested. This by no means implies a change in the immutable Brahman. As we have said earlier, when the waves rise in the ocean, the ocean does not increase; when they subside, the ocean does not decrease. Count the number of all the atoms in all the universes, all of those numbers have arisen from infinity without reducing the infinity by even an infinitesimal fraction. The many manifestations of phenomena arising out of what some ancient Greek philosophers first termed the great noumenon beyond do not produce any alterations whatsoever in the noumenon itself.

The philosophy of difference between Brahman and the *Karana Ishvara* must be carefully understood, however. In Brahman there is not even the slightest stirring toward phenomena. In *Karana Ishvara,* God the primal cause, the principle of causation is established. That is, God himself now *wills* to be the cause of the *forthcoming* universe. *Hiranya-garbha Ishvara*, the golden womb, is God within the universe. In other words, having created the universe, God now dwells in it. The golden womb is the spirit that makes phenomena holy and sacred; it is the teaching spirit of the universe. All intuitive knowledge, inspiration and revelation come into the soul because of its link with the golden womb, and yogis initiate their disciples so as to reestablish their connection with this holy spirit. From the golden womb all the diverse phenomena are created. These are as limbs in the body of God. Here God, the spirit, views the universe as we view our own individual bodies. The best description of God as *Virat* is to be found in the ninth, tenth and eleventh chapters of the Bhagavad Gita, and the reader is strongly advised to refer to these highly inspiring and elevating chapters.

*Ishvara* at all these three levels is the personal God who has a definite relationship with the universe and with whom we have a daily relationship. At the *Virat* level all the evolutions and histories of the galaxies, suns, planets and species have already begun, and from this *Virat* proceed the three principles: Brahma, Vishnu and Shiva—the God who creates the universe; the God in whom it subsists, continues and is preserved; and the God into whom it is finally dissolved. The Vishnu and the Shiva principles incarnate, become flesh, and the incarnations are known as the *avataras*, of whom we have spoken earlier. Smaller sparks from *Virat* (and from the three conscious principles of creation, preservation and dissolution operating the various forces of nature) are termed *devas*, the shining ones. These are all, as it were, flames in the one cosmic fire of consciousness, *chid-agni*.

Having discussed the universal, we now come to the individual soul. In some systems of philosophy the soul is eternally self-existent. In Sankhya there is some ambivalence about it. There is the great universal soul and the individual soul, but whether or not the individual souls are sparks of the great universal has not been clearly stated in the Sankhya philosophy. It is left entirely to the seeker to discover the true nature of the soul through the practice of yoga and meditation. In the Vedanta system individual souls are definitely considered to be sparks of Brahman. Each has its own cycle of duties to be fulfilled and truths to be discovered. The goal in both systems of philosophy remains the discovery of the true self, and the Vedanta is emphatic in repeatedly stating, "Thou art That." Through their association with *prakrti*, of which we will speak later, the various *jivas*, the life sparks, or individual souls, develop their own *karma*. They may be born as human beings, they may fall to lower stages, they may rise to higher human states, or they may even ascend to the state of the *devas*, the shining ones (these shining ones may either be descended from *Ishvara* or they may achieve their status by ascending from human souls). Then, when human beings have attained *samadhi* and have freed themselves from the *karmic* delimitations caused by ignorance of their own true nature, they become *jivan-muktas*, or *siddhas*, the accomplished ones, the adepts, the perfected ones. There is no difference between an *avatara* and a *siddha*. An *avatara* has descended from the divine being, a *siddha* has ascended from human status; but having come to the same rung of the ladder of spiritual evolution, or devolution, both enjoy the same stature in the universal order.

The spiritual force of the divine power manifests itself in many forms. The causal God, the golden womb, the universal soul, the conscious principles called Vishnu and Shiva (or their incarnations), together with the *devas*, may all manifest themselves:

By assuming a body of flesh and dwelling among living beings.

By assuming a body of pure energy which may seem like a fleshy being but which is in fact simply a vortex of force without any solid attributes.

By *avesha*, or working through the consciousness of an embodied soul so that for the duration of this *avesha* the particular personality assumes divine stature and power.

By making an appearance at holy celebrations such as the Eucharist or at holy places and sacred spots where devotees have established an altar and have sincerely invited the great spirit to be present.

This by no means exhausts the list, for God's powers are many and His manifestations innumerable. Yet like the Christian holy trinity, all of these manifestations are one; the one proceeds from infinity, dwells in infinity and returns to infinity.

From *Ishvara* downwards it appears, from the way language is used, that God assumes a masculine role. This is not necessarily so. God is genderless. Whether or not one's path goes through the universal masculine or the universal feminine polarity depends upon the seeker, or devotee. Both the texts and the tradition pay homage to *Shakti* or *Devi* (the feminine shining one), and for each of the above masculine terms there are feminine counterparts. It is even said in a hymn, "Without the innate femininity, the Lord is impotent." Both the words *potentia* and *shakti* are feminine, and all the terms for energy and sacred power in the Sanskrit language are feminine.

For a fuller understanding of the scheme, from Brahman to here, please see Chart I (see page 126). Chart II (see page 127) briefly illustrates the Sankhya scheme starting from *purusha* (*atman* of the Vedanta) and *Prakriti*.

*Prakriti*, as explained earlier, is often identified with the *maya* of Vedanta, for the principle of the development of the objective phenomena begins from *prakriti*, and it is here that the three *gunas* first develop. In other words, *prakriti* is the three-stranded rope that serves as an instrument of bondage for the individuated conscious principle which thereby becomes a personal God or a person. The three *gunas* of *prakriti* are well-known, but, briefly, they are:

*Sattva*, the principle of harmony, purity and light, symbolized by the color white;

*Rajas*, the principle of activity, movement, energy, symbolized by the color red;

*Tamas*, the principle of inertia, stability or stagnation, darkness, symbolized by the color black.

For a deeper understanding of these three principles, the readers are strongly urged to study Chapters 14, 17-18 of the Bhagavad Gita.

These three principles, or *gunas*, exist as unmanifest, in total equilibrium in the original *prakriti*. Only when the presence of the conscious person stirs up the inner core of *prakriti*, and the equilibrium is disturbed, do the three *gunas* begin to interact with each other. Then, combined with the two polarities within the power of *maya* (veiling and projecting), these three *gunas* produce all the objective material phenomena of the universe. *Prakriti* thus provides a body for the spirit that is either the personal God or the person. Not all of *prakriti*, however, serves to become the objective universe. Much of it remains in a pure relationship to serve as the body of *Karana-Ishvara*, God

# CHART I

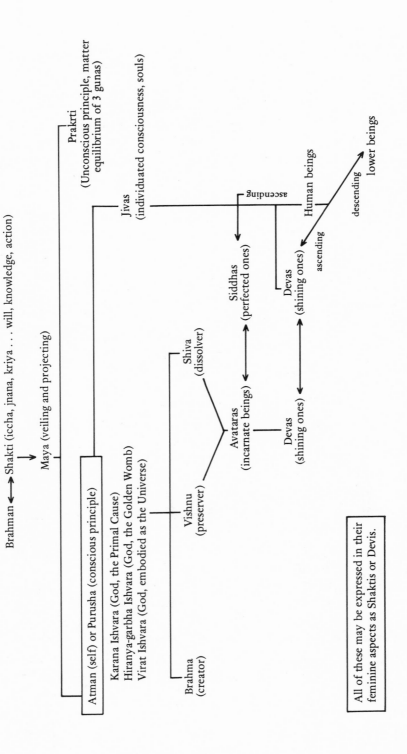

Brahman ←→ Shakti (iccha, jnana, kriya . . . will, knowledge, action)

Maya (veiling and projecting)

Prakrti
(Unconscious principle, matter
equilibrium of 3 gunas)

Atman (self) or Purusha (conscious principle)

Karana Ishvara (God, the Primal Cause)
Hiranya-garbha Ishvara (God, the Golden Womb)
Virat Ishvara (God, embodied as the Universe)

Brahma
(creator)

Vishnu
(preserver)

Shiva
(dissolver)

Avataras
(incarnate beings)

Siddhas
(perfected ones)

Devas
(shining ones)

Devas
(shining ones)

Jivas
(individuated consciousness, souls)

ascending

Human beings

descending

ascending

lower beings

All of these may be expressed in their
feminine aspects as Shaktis or Devis.

# CHART II

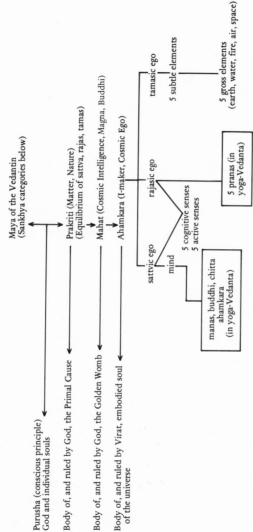

Maya of the Vedantin
(Sankhya categories below)

Purusha (conscious principle)
God and individual souls

Prakriti (Matter, Nature)
(Equilibrium of sattva, rajas, tamas)

Body of, and ruled by God, the Primal Cause

Mahat (Cosmic Intelligence, Magna, Buddhi)

Body of, and ruled by God, the Golden Womb

Ahamkara (I-maker, Cosmic Ego)

Body of, and ruled by Virat, embodied soul
of the universe

sattvic ego

mind

5 cognitive senses
5 active senses

manas, buddhi, chitta
ahamkara
(in yoga-Vedanta)

rajasic ego

5 pranas (in
yoga-Vedanta)

tamasic ego

5 subtle elements

5 gross elements
(earth, water, fire, air, space)

Notes:

1.  The Vedanta philosophy incorporates the major Sankhya categories; Sankhya does not include the Brahman-principle and its devolutes.

2.  The right column shows the evolutes of the Unconscious Principle (according to the Sankhya school); it depicts the material cause of the universe.

3.  The left column shows the individuated devolution of the Conscious Principle, assuming lower identities (according to Vedanta); it depicts the efficient cause of the universe.

4.  Philosophers of the *Nyaya-Vaisheshika* school discuss only nine entities; earth, water, fire, air, space, time, dimension, mind, soul (and God). Their system, developed approximately from the 7th century B.C. to the 17th century A.D., is very similar to the theology of Saint Thomas Aquinas; their arguments in favor of the existence of God bear remarkable similarity to that of Christian theologians.

the primal cause. Even though the universe is in a state of disequilibrium, inside it a force of the equilibrium of *prakriti* remains, and at the end of a cycle of creation the universe (which is in a state of disequilibrium) returns to a state of equilibrium again.

As the primal cause devolves to become the golden womb, the stirrings in *prakriti* produce *mahat*, the *magna*, the first mass that is trying to find an identity, or sets of identities. In purely scientific terms it may be thought of as that nebulous state of matter from which the vortices of energy, called the atomic particles, are later produced and into which these vortices again dissolve. The union of the golden womb and the *mahat* creates the most important principle in the cosmic personality—the universal *buddhi*, or cosmic consciousness, which has an identity as a universal person. All the later beings partake of this *buddhi*. Without this "vast" *mahat*, cosmic intelligence, no further individuation (which is like vortices developing in the cosmic waters of both the conscious and unconscious principles) can take place.

From *mahat* proceeds the principle of *ahamkara*, the I-maker. This is the cosmic ego, and it is here that the process of false identification fully crystallizes. Here, the personality begins to say, This is "I," when it refers to the material body, assuming names and forms, possessing delimited attributes as opposed to the unlimited, unmanifest power. But the Virat truly knows the universe to be His body, and all the suns, planets and galaxies to be, as it were, His hands, feet and mouth.

From the *sattvic* aspects of *prakriti*, the shining ones derive their bodies. The *sattvic* ego, known as *vaikarika*, produces the mind. Some authorities believe that the cognitive senses (the abilities of sight, sound, touch, taste, and smell, as well as the abilities of the active senses whose powers are seen in the human body in the hands, feet and organs of speech, generation and elimination) are also produced from the same *sattvic* ego. All authorities agree that the *tamasic* ego, called *bhutadi*, produces the five subtle elements (*tan matras*—to be explained below). All authorities also agree that the *rajasic* ego is responsible for the movement necessary in order for the *sattvic* and *tamasic* egos to produce their effects. Some authorities, however, believe that mind alone is produced from the *sattvic* ego and that the *rajasic* ego produces the cognitive and the active senses. (See Chart II, page 127.)

Anything in the universe that has a tangible form, a gross appearance, first has a counterpart in the subtle, more refined, world. For instance, the five subtle elements, the *tan-matras*, are the refined principles behind our awareness of sight, sound, touch, taste and smell, which then become actual, objective experiences through the contact of the senses. From these *matras* (from which the word *matter* may have been derived) evolve the five gross elements: earth, water, fire, air and space. These words do not signify the planet Earth and the flowing water and so forth, but rather they represent the way our psychology perceives the universe in its five states of matter as well as the five states of matter, themselves. In other words, the solid, liquid, combustive and luminous, gaseous and the spatial states of matter are meant by the term, gross elements. Space is not regarded as simply emptiness; it is an actual state of matter.

This is the plan of the phenomena that develop through the interaction of *sattva, rajas* and *tamas* between the positive and negative polarities. All the objects of the world, all the physical or chemical states of matter as well as our mental attitudes toward them are constituted of these, and none other. (The *Nyaya-Vaisheshika*, for instance, the philosophers of logical atomism, who were responsible for developing theories about the physical universe, took into account, for their purpose, only nine entities: earth, water, fire, air, space, time, dimension, soul and the mind.)

All these levels of individuation and evolution are the *upadhis*, attributed as conditions of that which is ultimately non-qualitative, and it is through the process of conditioning that the *nir-guna*, the non-qualitative, becomes *saguna*, qualitative, endowed with *gunas*. This is also known as the process of *adhyaropa*, or superimposition. According to this process, the universe is superimposed onto God, just as the appearance of silver is superimposed onto a glinting seashell. When the superimposition is eradicated through the process of right knowledge, the liberation of that which was never bound is "re-cognized."

Highly complex relationships that exist between the conscious and the unconscious worlds are defined in these terms:

> Two polarities
> Trinity of Godhood (Causal, Golden Womb, Virat)
>   in relation to *prakriti*, *mahat* and *ahamkara*, respectively
> Five cosmic sheaths
> Five individual sheaths
> Three cosmic bodies
> Three individual bodies

The false identification that exists between the limited conditioning placed by the material world on the one hand, and the thus-conditioned conscious principle on the other, can be broken only through the practice of meditation and total surrender to that divine nature which permeates and fills us and is never far away.

For an exposition of the relationships that exist between the subtle and the gross worlds and among the states of consciousness, sheaths and bodies of the individual and the cosmic beings, we present some passages from an introductory text, *Vedantasara*, of the yogi Sadananda, a monk of the Shankaracharya order who lived in the fifteenth century.

> 1. Superimposition means attributing to the real the nature of the unreal. The real is the non-dual Brahman—existence-consciousness-bliss. All the unconscious principles such as ignorance are unreal.
>
> Ignorance* of the true reality is described as positive; it is the opposite of knowledge, consisting of the three *gunas*, separate from both being and non-being, but undefinable.
>
> 2. This ignorance may be treated as one (universal, collective), or manifold, depending on whether it is pertaining to the universal aggregate or to the indivual. Just as many trees, taken collectively, are termed *a forest*, or many waters coming together, *a reservoir*, so in the case of the souls appearing as *many*, collective ignorance is common. This universal ignorance, a condition associated with a higher being, has the predominance of pure *sattva*.
>
> 3. The consciousness conditioned by such (cosmic) ignorance is signified as *Ishvara*, the personal God, the cause of the universe, the all-pervading, unmanifest, endowed with qualities such as omniscience, omnipotence, all-controlling power; He is

---

*For a clear definition of the term *ignorance* in this context, please see above, page 120. The reader is advised not to read this summary further without grasping the definition of ignorance.

so-called because He is the illuminator of all ignorance; that is, all the lower states are illuminated by the light of this higher one.

4. This universal ignorance in the personal God, *Ishvara*, is termed the universal causal body because it is the cause of all; it is called the *sheath of bliss (anandamaya kosha)** because of its profusion of happiness, and because it covers reality like a sheath. It is the state of cosmic sleep, as all else ceases here. For the same reason it is called the place where all the gross and the subtle schema *(prapaneha)* dissolves.

5. Just as a single forest, seen as its manifold components, is termed "trees," or just as a reservoir is made up of many waters, so universal ignorance is expressed as manifold with reference to individuated beings. This individual ignorance, a condition in association with a lower being, has the predominance of stained *sattva*.

6. The consciousness conditioned by such ignorance is called *prajna* (because of its limited knowledge and because it is the subject of attributes such as "devoid of lordship").

7. Because it is the original cause of ego *(ahamkara)*, *prajna* is called the (individual) causal body; it is also called the sheath of bliss because of the profusion of pleasure and because it covers reality like a sheath. It is the state of (individual) sleep, as all else ceases here. For the same reason it is called the place into which the experience of the gross and the subtle bodies dissolves.

---

* This is not to be confused with the bliss of Brahman; it is the limitation placed upon it through ignorance, as in the pleasure of sleep.

8.   In this state both *Ishvara* (the personal God) and *prajna* (the ignorant soul) experience pleasure from the very subtle waves of ignorance which are illuminated by consciousness; this is seen when a person, waking from a sleep observes, "I had such a pleasant sleep. I knew nothing." (Obviously he has enjoyed the "pleasure" of ignorance which is illuminated by consciousness, without which he would not have been able to make an observation about his sleep.)

9.   These cosmic and individual principles of ignorance are mutually identical, like the forest and the trees, or the reservoir and the waters.

10. Just as the space enclosed by the forest and the trees is identical, and just as the reflection of the sky in a reservoir or in the various waters is the same, so *Ishvara* (the personal God) and the ignorant *jiva* (soul) conditioned by this ignorance are yet identical.

11. The superconscious nature *(Turiya*, the fourth state beyond wakefulness, dream or sleep) is like that undelimited, unconditioned space which is the vast substratum of both the spaces occupied by a limited forest or the trees therein, or like the sky which is reflected in a reservoir or in the various waters. Both the limited spaces are merely a delimiting condition placed on the vast indivisible space. The superconscious nature is the substratum of both the cosmic and the individual ignorance as well as of the personal God *(Ishvara)* and the individuated soul *(prajna)* who are both as delimiting conditions placed on the indivisible superconscious.

12. This fourth state, pure superconsciousness, when not discriminated from the delimited consciousness that is conditioned by ignorance and so forth, is

like a red-hot iron ball in which the fire and the iron cannot be separated; it is the implied meaning of the great dictum: "That Thou Art."

13. Ignorance *(maya)* has twofold power: the power to veil and the power to project. The power to veil is like a cloud which, though small, can obstruct the sun. So ignorance, though limited, as it were, covers the capacity of the undelimited Self, *(atman)*, which is not of this world; it does so by obstructing the intelligence *(buddhi)* of the observer. When the *atman* is covered by this veil it begins to consider the possibility of being an actor and experiencer, being happy, unhappy, etc., just as a rope may appear to be a snake when the observer's view is affected by ignorance.

14. The power of projection is like ignorance about the rope. This ignorance, by a power inherent within itself, gives rise to the false perception of a snake in the rope. Similarly, ignorance, by a power inherent within itself, gives rise to a capacity to produce within the self (which is veiled by it), the schema of space, etc. The power of projection creates the entire universe, starting from *linga* (that is the subtle bodies), and progressing to the whole universe.

15. Consciousness conditioned by ignorance (which has the power both to veil and to project) serves as the efficient cause when its own self is dominant; it serves as the material cause when the *upadhis* (limitations or conditionings) are predominant. It is like the spider which, by its own self, is the efficient cause, but who, taking into account the use of its body, is the material cause of the web.

16. Space is born from consciousness conditioned

by ignorance using the power of projection in which *tamas* is dominant, and from this proceed air and all the other elements. These elements, which when uncompounded are merely the subtle measure of the gross elements, are called subtle elements *(tanmatras)*, and from these subtle elements the subtle bodies and gross elements are produced.

17. The subtle bodies are called *linga-sharira* (literally, trace bodies) and have seventeen components: the five cognitive senses, the five active senses, the five *pranas*, intelligence—*buddhi* and the mind—*manas.* (*Chitta*—mind-stuff—and *ahamkara*—ego— are included in the intelligence and mind.) These, *manas, buddhi, chitta* and *ahamkara*, because they are luminous, are considered to be products of the *sattvic* particles of the elements.

18. The *buddhi* (intelligence), combined with the cognitive senses, is called the sheath of limited knowledge, the *vijnanamaya kosha* because it covers reality like a sheath. Through this sheath the individuated self has developed a false identification with pragmatic reality, as though it were a doer, an experiencer, having pleasure or pain, migrating through this world and the next.

19. The mind, combined with the cognitive senses, is called the mental sheath, *manomaya kosha.*

20. The five *pranas*, combined with the active senses, comprise the *prana* sheath (the *pranamaya kosha*). Because of their active nature, these are said to be the effects of the powers of projection in which *rajas* is dominant.

21. Among these sheaths, the *vijnanamaya* inheres the *jnana-shakti*, Brahman's power of knowledge; it

is the agent of action and causation. The *manomaya* sheath inheres in it *iccha-shakti* (the Brahman's will); it is the instrument of action and causation. The *pranamaya* sheath inheres in itself the *kriya-shakti* ( Brahman's power of action); it is the effect of the action and causation. This division of the sheaths, the teachers say, is based on their efficacy. These three sheaths, together, are called the subtle body. (See Chart III, page 138).

22. In this regard the subtle body of all is single, universal, like the forest or the reservoir when thought of as one, or it may pertain to each individual separately like trees or individual waters when thought of as manifold.

23. This consciousness, when considered in its universal condition, is also called *sutra-atman* (one thread of all selves), the golden womb and the universal *prana*, because it is threaded through all, and in it inheres the power of knowledge, will and action.

24. The universal aggregate of the three sheaths (the *vijnanamaya, manomaya* and *pranamaya*) is subtler in comparison to the gross schema, and it is therefore termed the place into which the gross schema is brought to dissolution.

25. This same consciousness, when considered to be conditioned by the individual, is termed *taijasa*, effulgent, because it is associated with the inner sense, that of mental processes, which is illuminated by consciousness. This individual condition consisting of the three *koshas—vijnanamaya, manomaya* and *pranamaya—*is subtler than the gross body, and it is therefore called the individual subtle body. It is also called the dream state because it carries

impressions from the wakeful state and is designated as the place into which the gross body is dissolved.

26. The *sutra-atman* (the universal subtle body) and *taijasa* (the effulgent individual subtle body) experience the subtle operations of the mind in that state. Like the unlimited space artificially delimited through a division between the forest and the trees, like the sky reflecting in the reservoir or in the waters, these universal and individual subtle bodies, *sutra-atman* and *taijasa*, are inseparable, one in the superconscious.

27. The gross elements (earth, water, fire, air, space), together with their attributes (sound, touch, form, taste and smell), are variously compounded with their gross objects and the gross bodies of different living beings, depending on whether one looks with a view to universal oneness or to the individuality. The gross body of all may be either a single universal or a separate individual, as in the previous example of the forest and the trees, the reservoir and the waters. This consciousness, when in the condition of a single universal, is termed *Vaishvanara*, the single aggregate universal personality, or *Virat*, the vast luminous personality, because it assumes its identity through all persons and because it shines in the manifestation of the universal phenomena in diverse manners.

28. The universal gross body is called the *annamaya* sheath. It is made up of food because it is a product of the gross phenomena of the objective world which are, as it were, food that is consumed by God when they are dissolved. It is called the wakeful (and the gross) body because it is the medium for the experience of gross objects.

## CHART III

| BODY | COMPOSED OF | EQUIVALENT KOSHA (SHEATH) |
|---|---|---|
| Karana Sharira | Maya or Prakriti | Anandamaya, sheath of the bliss of ignorance |
| Linga Sharira or Sukshma Sharira Subtle Body (trace body) | 1. Manas (active mind) ⎫ These two include<br>2. Buddhi (intelligence) ⎬ Chitta (cosmic mind-<br> ⎭ stuff) and Ahamkara (ego) | Vijnanamaya, sheath of delimited knowledge; buddhi (intelligence) combined with cognitive senses |
| | 3. Powers of the five cognitive senses | Manomaya, sheath of mental processes; mind combined with cognitive senses |
| | 4. Powers of the five active senses<br>5. Five pranas, fields of vitality | Pranamaya, sheath of vital processes; force fields of vitality combined with the active senses |
| Sthula Sharira Gross Body | Physical elements | Annamaya, sheath composed of what is absorbed by the consumption of food |

# CHART IV

BRAHMAN (Existence-Consciousness-Bliss)
Infinite, Absolute, Transcendental; Transpersonal; Without qualifications, without quantum or attributes. NIRGUNA

TURIYA → Unaltered consciousness, SUPERCONSCIOUSNESS

→ Contains MAYA which veils the Infinity; projects finiteness

SAGUNA CONSCIOUSNESS, delimited, qualified, superimposed.

**SUPERIMPOSITIONS on BRAHMAN:**

→ KARANA ISHVARA: God the Primal Cause:
The Infinite has become One; the Transcendental now ready to create the empirical universe; the Absolute entering into relation-ship with the relative.

→ HIRANYA-GARBHA ISHVARA:
Golden Womb or
SUTRATMA PRANA: Life-thread running through the universe and through all the souls
Holy Spirit
One becoming many
The teaching spirit
That which sanctifies

→ VIRAT ISHVARA: The embodied universal spirit or
VAISHVANARA: The unitary person-ality of all personalities
Regards the universe as His body; the many limbs of this universal body belong to the one spirit. (See Bhagavad Gita, chapters 9-11).

See the following chart for their corresponding: Aspects of Prakriti embodied, Body, Sheath, Guna, States of Conscious-ness with reference to the Cosmic Consciousness principle, as well as to the individuated consciousness (jivas, souls).

# CHART V

BRAHMAN

SAGUNA (delimited, qualified)

| | KARANA ISHVARA | HIRANYA-GARBHA | VIRAT ISHVARA |
|---|---|---|---|
| GOD'S CONSCIOUSNESS NAMED | KARANA ISHVARA: God the Primal Cause: The Infinite has become One; the Transcendental now ready to create the empirical universe; the Absolute entering into relationship with the relative. | HIRANYA-GARBHA ISHVARA: Golden Womb or SUTRATMA PRANA: Life-thread running through the universe and through all the souls. Holy Spirit One becoming many The Teaching spirit That which sanctifies | VIRAT ISHVARA: The embodied universal spirit or VAISHVANARA: The unitary personality of all personalities. Regards the universe as His body; the many limbs of this universal body belong to the one spirit. (See Bhagavad Gita, chapters 9-11). AHAMKARA: the cosmic ego; the instrument by which indivual identities are established in consciousness; the I-maker. |
| ASPECT OF PRAKRTI EMBODIED | PRAKRITI: equilibrium of the 3 gunas | MAHAT: the first evolute; magna, cosmic buddhi (intelligence) | |
| BODY | KARANA SHARIRA Cosmic Causal Body | LINGA SHARIRA or Sukshma Sharira Cosmic Subtle Body | STHULA SHARIRA Cosmic Gross Body |
| SHEATH | ANANDAMAYA KOSHA: Sheath of the bliss of ignorance that is no longer the Transcendental Brahman; Brahman becoming the Personal God. | VIJNANAMAYA KOSHA: Sheath of delimited cognition MANOMAYA KOSHA: Sheath of mental processes PRANAMAYA KOSHA: Sheath of vital processes. | ANNAMAYA KOSHA: Sheath made of food (which is the universe that is again consumed at the end of a cycle of creation). |
| GUNA | Pure sattva | rajas | tamas |

SAGUNA GOD IN COSMIC CONSCIOUSNESS

| | | | |
|---|---|---|---|
| STATE OF CONSCIOUSNESS | Cosmic sleep; the universe has not yet been created; lies dormant. | Cosmic dream | Cosmic awakening |
| CORRESPONDING STATES OF CONSCIOUSNESS | PRAJNA (of delimited knowledge) | TAIJASA: effulgent, luminous (like the luminosity in a dream where our ignorance of ourselves yet reflects the light of the conscious self) | VISHVA, the entered one (the subtle body having entered the gross body) |
| BODY | KARANA SHARIRA Individual causal body | LINGA or SUKSHMA SHARIRA Individual subtle body; repository of all experiences, actions, impressions, samskaras, karmas and their fruition; vehicle of reincarnation. | STHULA SHARIRA Individual physical body; created at individual's conception, dissolved at death. |
| SHEATH | ANANDAMAYA KOSHA: Sheath of bliss | VIJNANAMAYA KOSHA: Sheath of delimited knowledge. MANOMAYA KOSHA: Sheath of mental processes. PRANAMAYA KOSHA: Sheath of vital processes | ANNAMAYA KOSHA: Sheath composed of food |
| GUNA | Stained sattva | rajas | tamas |
| CONSCIOUSNESS EXPERIENCED | Individual sleep; asleep to one's own nature | Individual dream | Individual wakefulness |

CORRESPONDING INDIVIDUATED CONSCIOUSNESS; JIVAS (souls)

29. The same consciousness, when in the condition of individuated beings, is termed *vishva*, that which enters, because it has entered the gross body without relinquishing ego-identity with the subtle body. This is the individual gross body, and it is called the wakeful *annamaya* sheath because it is made up of food. There is no differentiation between the individual and universal gross bodies, the *vishva* and *vaishvanara*; they are one, as is the delimited space conditioned by the delimitations of the forest and the trees, or the sky reflected in the reservoir or the waters.

30. Just as the gross, subtle and causal bodies each constitute universal, as well as individual bodies, so do these three *together* also form a single universe, like a great forest that is made up of many smaller forests or like one great reservoir that is made up of many reservoirs together. The consciousness conditioned by this, from *Vaishvanara* to *Ishvara*, too, is all one, like undelimited space conditioned by the delimitations of the subforests, or like little reservoirs constituting a larger reservoir. This consciousness, when not conditioned by the great schema, when not discriminated like the hot iron ball (see pages 131-132), is signified by the great dictum, "All this is Brahman."

Let us simplify these Vedanta categories as follows:

*BRAHMAN*, in whom *maya* dwells, is the absolute transcendental.

*MAYA* has two powers—to veil and to project.

*MAYA* subdivides into conscious *(Ishvara, atman, purusha)* and unconscious *(prakriti)* principles.

The CONSCIOUS principle becomes God (three-fold: *Karana*, *Hiranya-garbha* and *Virat*) and the souls.

The UNCONSCIOUS principle provides the body—universal and individual.

*Karana Ishvara*, God the primal cause, has *prakriti* (the equilibrium of the three *gunas*) as its body; it is referred to as the universal causal body; wearing the *(anandamaya)* sheath of the bliss of ignorance, it is delimited (no longer Brahman), conditioned to create the universe, dwelling in cosmic sleep. The cosmic consciousness at this level is purely *sattvic.* The individual *jivas* (souls) at this consciousness level are called *prajna* (of delimited knowledge); wearing the individual causal body and the sheath of bliss, dwelling in individual sleep, their consciousness is of *sattva* which has become stained.

*Hiranya-garbha*, the golden womb, or *sutratman* (one thread of the spirit) has the *mahat* state of *prakriti's* evolute as its body; referred to as the universal subtle body (which consists of three cosmic sheaths—*Vijnanamanya, manomaya, pranamaya*), dwelling in cosmic dreams, its consciousness is *rajasic.*

The individual *jivas* (souls) at this consciousness level are called *taijasa* (effulgent) because consciousness reflects on their ignorance; wearing the individual dreams, their consciousness is *rajasic.*

The subtle body consists of: (1) mind—*manas*; (2) intelligence—*buddhi* (these first two include *chitta*, the mind-stuff, and *ahamkara*, the ego); (3) the five cognitive senses; (4) the five active senses and (5) the five *pranas*. The subtle body is an aggregate of three sheaths:

The *vijnanamaya* sheath (of limited cognition) consists of *buddhi* combined with the cognitive senses, with Brahman's power of knowledge dominant. This causes the self to consider himself an *agent* of actions and causation.

The *manomaya* sheath of the mind consists of the mind, combined with the cognitive senses, with Brahman's power of will dominant. This causes the self to consider itself an *instrument* of actions and causation while controlling the instruments.

The *pranamaya* sheath of vitality consists of the *pranas* combined with the active senses, with Brahman's power of action dominant. This causes the self to consider itself the *effect* of action and causation.

*Virat* or *Vaishvanara*, the universal embodied soul, has *ahamkara*, the cosmic ego, as its body; referred to as the universal gross body, wearing the *annamaya* sheath made up of food, and dwelling in cosmic wakefulness, the cosmic consciousness at this level is *tamasic*. The individual *jivas* (souls) at this consciousness level are called *vishva*—the subtle body having entered the gross body, wearing the individual sheath made of food. Their consciousness is dominated by *tamas*.

Here we end the passages from the yogi Sadananda's work, *Vedantasara*, and summarize more of his argument (which closely follows Shankara's view) below:

Let us explain how the ignorant manage to superimpose on the innermost self ideas such as, "I am this, I am this" and so forth. The very naive may enter into a relationship and say, for example, "My son is my own self. When he is nourished, I feel nourished. When he is lost,

I am lost." Among such people there are some who would leave that same son burning in a blazing house and later declare their own physical body, rather than the son, to be the true self, saying, "I am slim. I am fat." Thus they assume the physical body to be the self. Some consider the senses to be the self. They see that, in the absence of the senses, the body does not go on, and one says, "I am blind. I am deaf." Some think that *prana* is the self, saying, "When I am hungry or thirsty, my personality is weakened because the *prana* is weak." Up to here we have represented the various materialist views.

Some go further into the subtleties of the personality and have reached the point at which they think that the mind is the self. They say, "When the mind is asleep, the senses and *pranas* are dormant, and I know myself to be oscillating between the ideas of pro and con." Observing these functions of the mind, they consider that to be the self. Some go deeper, up to the *vijnanamaya* sheath, and say, "When an agent is absent, the instrument is inefficacious, and since I experience myself to be the agent and the experiencer, it is the intelligence, the *buddhi*, which is the self." This is said to be the Buddhist view. As our realization grows further we join the company of those who identify themselves with the *anandamaya* sheath. They observe that the intelligence and so forth are ultimately dissolved into a state of ignorance and begin to feel, "I am ignorant. I am without knowledge." Thus they consider ignorance to be the self. This is the view of the logicians and of the philosopher, Prabhakara, of the *Mimamsa* school.

Yet there are others who state that we do not see presence or absence of light in deep sleep, who say, "In that state I do not know myself." On the basis of this experience the self is to be defined as consciousness conditioned by ignorance. This view is held by the philosopher, Kumarila, of the *Mimamsa* school, a senior contemporary of Shankara. A different school of Buddhists states that there is the total absence of anything in deep sleep. "When one wakes up from sleep," they say, "it is almost as though he has ceased to exist. On the basis of this it is safe to say that *atman* is *shunya, nihil*."

The yogi Sadananda says that in this manner we gradually eliminate the experience of any identification with the grosser in favor of the finer, and yet finer, until we go to that which illuminates all of these levels of awareness—that which is not gross, not an agent, which is pure consciousness, without cognitive senses, without *prana*, without mind, by nature ever-pure, ever-wise, ever-free. That inward consciousness alone is the reality of the Self.

We must constantly strive to elevate our consciousness above the level of superimposition and to free ourselves from the false identifications that have been established by the delimited ego. This *apavada*, de-superimposition, can occur only through proper, deep contemplation, or meditation, in which we trace each grosser level to its finer source and each individuated conditioning to its universal unity, ultimately merging the entire schema into the great superconscious Brahman.

Sadananda ends his text with these words:

> When one has attained the final God-realization he has reached *kaivalya*, absoluteness and *jivan-mukti*, liberation, while still embodied. Such a person continues to function, simply maintaining the body for the fulfilment of its purpose—to complete the ripening of the fruits such as pleasure and pain from the *karmas* already performed that have begun to bear fruit—but initiating no new *karmas*. This fruition, the experience of pain and pleasure arising from *karma*,

may be a result of his own will at times, but he experiences them as his soul illuminates all that is being reflected into the inner sense of his mind. When he has completed the fruition, it ceases. His senses and *prana* are then absorbed in Brahman, and there is no further need even for truth, or knowledge, or for the causes to be undertaken as a result of knowledge, or for the impressions (the *samskaras*) to be activated by such acts. There then remains supreme absoluteness, completely devoid of any reflection of difference, the unitary Brahman.

In this work we have attempted to inquire into the nature of God and have presented the position that the ancient tradition of yoga-Vedanta takes in order to bring all divergent ideas together. Now we will quote from hymns composed by the great Sanskrit poet, Kalidasa, known as the Shakespeare of India, and if you look at the following verses with care, you will end this reading in a contemplative frame of mind.

The poet Kalidasa sings:

The shining ones fell at his feet and addressed their praises
To him who is the pacifier of their enemies,
The one to whom praises are due,
Who is beyond the grasp of speech or mind.

Salutations to you who first creates, then bears and then
Withdraws the world, you whose self abides thus threefold.
Just as the rain water, naturally sweet, takes on other
Tastes when falling at various places, so also you, by nature
Immutable, take up various conditions
In (conjunction with) the *gunas*.

Immeasurable, you measure the worlds,
Seeking nothing, you grant what is sought.
Unconquered, you are victorious,
And entirely unmanifest, you are the cause
of the manifest.

They (the wise) know you as living in the heart, yet distant,
Free of desires, yet practicing asceticism,

Compassionate, yet untouched by sin,
Ancient, yet free of decay.

Omniscient, you are unknown,
Origin of all, you are self-existent;
Lord of all, you are masterless,
Though one, you divide into all forms.

They say that you are sung of in the seven *samans*,
You rest in the waters of seven oceans,
You have in your mouth the seven fires
And you are the sole support of seven worlds.

From you who have four faces (arises) knowledge
With its fourfold fruit
(Laws of virtue, material life, desires and liberation)
And the four states of time (the four *yugas*—aeons),
As well as the people with their fourfold divisions of *varnas*
    (social duties).

For emancipation the *yogins*
With mind controlled by practice
Concentrate on you who are the light
Living in (their) hearts.

Who knows the true reality of you?
You take birth, though unborn,
You destroy the evil, though without movement,
You are asleep, yet ever wakeful.

Yours is the power to enjoy the objects such as sound,
To observe the most difficult ascetic practices,
To guard (your) progeny
And yet remain a (neutral) witness.

Many paths, the ways to attainment,
Diversified by various teachings, all lead to you
As Ganga's floodwaters lead into the ocean.

For proper withdrawal (i.e. cessation of *samskara*)
You alone are the resort of those dispassionate ones
Whose minds have entered into you
And who have surrendered their actions to you.

Though you may be known by direct perception
Your glory is not limited
To (the forms of) this earth and such;

How can one state whether you are to be proved by inference
Or by the prophets' word of revelation?

Since you purify human beings
By their mere remembrance of you,
The fruits of all acts (and tendencies) are offerings unto you.

Like gems in the ocean, like splendors of the sun,
Your acts are beyond the power of any hymnal praise.

Nothing is unattained, yet to be attained, of you.
Only kindness towards the world is the reason
For your taking birth and performing actions.

Singing your glory if speech is silenced
It is through our weariness and incapacity
And not because this is the limit of your attributes.

*The Dynasty of Raghus, X, 15-32*

Then they (the shining ones) fell before him,
The sustainer of all,
The Lord of speech with faces in all directions,
And stood addressing him with meaningful words.

Salutations to you of three forms,
The absolute one self before creation,
Who then became divided,
Apportioning the three *gunas*.

As you sowed the unfailing seed in the waters
And from that arose the moving
And unmoving (things of) the world,
You are glorified as its source, O unborn one.

Though one, you emanate your power through three
    conditions,
Having become the cause of dissolution,
Continuity and creation.

Man and woman are your two halves as you split your form
With intent to create;
They are then the birth-givers of the creation
And are called its parents.

The sleeping and waking of you,
Whose nights and days
Are divided by the measure of your own time,
Is the dissolution and creation of things.


Without origin, you are the origin of the world;
Endless, the end of the world.
Beginningless, you are the beginning of the world;
Without a master, the lord of the world.


You know self by self, you create self by self;
With self having done the work
You dissolve back into the very self.
Liquid or compressed-solid, gross or subtle,
Light or heavy, manifest or otherwise
You make yourself as you wish.


You are the origin of speech which begins with Om,
Is changed with three pitch tones,
Has sacrifice as its application
And heaven as its fruit.


(The wise) consider you as nature (*prakrti*)
Which functions for the sake of the conscious principle
     (*purusa*);
The very you they also know as the person,
The neutral witness of *prakrti*.


You are father even of forefathers,
Deity of the deities,
Farther even than beyond
And ordainer even of ordainers.


You alone are the oblation as well as the priest,
The enjoyable and the eternal enjoyer;
Knowable and the knower,
The meditating one as well as
The supreme object of meditation.

*The Prince's Birth, II. 3-15.*

This is as close as we can come to describing God. Our true hymn is in silence; our true homage is in Om. Any questions unanswered will come to a resolution in deep meditation where all identities superimposed on Brahman simply cease, and only the infinite absolute remains. We close this discussion with passages from two ancient Sanskrit works:

1. Endowed with powers such as to become minute,
   With the crescent moon on his head,
   He bears the name *Lord, Ishvara*, not applicable to any other;

   He upholds this world with his eightfold self
   (of earth, water, fire, air, space, mind, intelligence, ego)
   Complementing each other's capacity
   As horses pull together a chariot;

   He is the force operating in the universe-field.
   On him the yogis are intent—and the wise say
   His place is free of the danger of return to the worldly cycle.

   He is the deity (*Shiva*) sleeping,
   Meditating within you.

2. He whom they call in the Vedanta One Person
       pervading both worlds;
   Whose title of *Lord, Ishvara*, applies to no other;
   For whom the seekers of deliverance search within,
       their vital breaths and such controlled;
   Who is found with ease through the yoga of devotion;
   May he, the absolute Lord, lead you to the supreme good.*

* The above poetry has appeared, in somewhat different form, in Usharbudh Arya, "Man in Kavya," *Literature East and West* (April, 1972) pp. 183-208.

The main building of the national headquarters, Honesdale, Pa.

# The Himalayan Institute

The Himalayan International Institute of Yoga Science and Philosophy of the U.S.A. is a nonprofit organization devoted to the scientific and spiritual progress of modern humanity. Founded in 1971 by Sri Swami Rama, the Institute combines Western and Eastern teachings and techniques to develop educational, therapeutic, and research programs for serving people in today's world. The goals of the Institute are to teach meditational techniques for the growth of individuals and their society, to make known the harmonious view of world religions and philosophies, and to undertake scientific research for the benefit of humankind.

This challenging task is met by people of all ages, all walks of life, and all faiths who attend and participate in the Institute courses and seminars. These programs, which are given on a continuing basis, are designed in order that one may discover for oneself how to live more creatively. In the words of Swami Rama, "By being aware of one's own potential and abilities, one can become a perfect citizen, help the nation, and serve humanity."

The Institute has branch centers and affiliates throughout the United States. The 422-acre campus of the national headquarters, located in the Pocono Mountains of northeastern Pennsylvania, serves as the coordination center for all the Institute activities, which include a wide variety of innovative programs in education, research, and therapy, combining Eastern and Western approaches to self-awareness and self-directed change.

SEMINARS, LECTURES, WORKSHOPS, and CLASSES are available throughout the year, providing intensive training and experience in such topics as Superconscious Meditation, hatha yoga, philosophy, psychology, and various aspects of personal growth and holistic health. The *Himalayan Institute Quarterly Guide to Classes and Other Offerings* is sent free of charge to everyone on the Institute's mailing list.

The RESIDENTIAL and SELF-TRANSFORMATION PROGRAMS provide training in the basic yoga disciplines— diet, ethical behavior, hatha yoga, and meditation. Students are also given guidance in a philosophy of living in a community environment.

The PROGRAM IN EASTERN STUDIES AND COM- PARATIVE PSYCHOLOGY offers a unique and systematic synthesis of Western empirical sources and Eastern introspective science. Masters and Doctoral-level studies may be pursued through cross-registration with several accredited colleges and universities.

The five-day STRESS MANAGEMENT/PHYSICAL FIT- NESS PROGRAM offers practical and individualized training that can be used to control the stress response. This includes biofeedback, relaxation skills, exercise, diet, breathing tech- niques, and meditation.

A yearly INTERNATIONAL CONGRESS, sponsored by the Institute, is devoted to the scientific and spiritual progress of modern humanity. Through lectures, workshops, seminars, and practical demonstrations, it provides a forum for professionals and lay people to share their knowledge and research.

The ELEANOR N. DANA RESEARCH LABORATORY is the psychophysiological laboratory of the Institute, specializing in research on breathing, meditation, holistic therapies, and stress and relaxed states. The laboratory is fully equipped for exercise stress testing and psychophysiological measurements, including brain waves, patterns of respiration, heart rate changes, and muscle tension. The staff investigates Eastern teachings through studies based on Western experimental techniques.

# Himalayan Institute Publications

| | |
|---|---|
| Living with the Himalayan Masters | Swami Rama |
| Lectures on Yoga | Swami Rama |
| A Practical Guide to Holistic Health | Swami Rama |
| Choosing a Path | Swami Rama |
| Inspired Thoughts of Swami Rama | Swami Rama |
| Freedom from the Bondage of Karma | Swami Rama |
| Book of Wisdom (Ishopanishad) | Swami Rama |
| Enlightenment Without God | Swami Rama |
| Exercise Without Movement | Swami Rama |
| Life Here and Hereafter | Swami Rama |
| Marriage, Parenthood, and Enlightenment | Swami Rama |
| Path of Fire and Light | Swami Rama |
| Perennial Psychology of the Bhagavad Gita | Swami Rama |
| Love Whispers | Swami Rama |
| Celestial Song/Gobind Geet | Swami Rama |
| Creative Use of Emotion | Swami Rama, Swami Ajaya |
| Science of Breath | Swami Rama, Rudolph Ballentine, M.D., Alan Hymes, M.D. |
| Yoga and Psychotherapy | Swami Rama, Rudolph Ballentine, M.D., Swami Ajaya |
| Yoga-sutras of Patanjali | Usharbudh Arya, D.Litt. |
| Superconscious Meditation | Usharbudh Arya, D.Litt. |
| Mantra and Meditation | Usharbudh Arya, D.Litt. |
| Philosophy of Hatha Yoga | Usharbudh Arya, D.Litt. |
| Meditation and the Art of Dying | Usharbudh Arya, D.Litt. |
| God | Usharbudh Arya, D.Litt. |
| Psychotherapy East and West: A Unifying Paradigm | Swami Ajaya, Ph.D. |
| Yoga Psychology | Swami Ajaya, Ph.D. |
| Psychology East and West | Swami Ajaya, Ph.D. (ed.) |
| Meditational Therapy | Swami Ajaya, Ph.D. (ed.) |
| Diet and Nutrition | Rudolph Ballentine, M.D. |
| Joints and Glands Exercises | Rudolph Ballentine, M.D. (ed.) |
| Theory and Practice of Meditation | Rudolph Ballentine, M.D. (ed.) |
| Freedom from Stress | Phil Nuernberger, Ph.D. |
| Science Studies Yoga | James Funderburk, Ph.D. |
| Homeopathic Remedies | Drs. Anderson, Buegel, Chernin |
| Hatha Yoga Manual I | Samskrti and Veda |